Never Judge a Book by its Cover
My Inspirational Journey to Success

Kalpna Suthar

NEVER JUDGE A BOOK BY ITS COVER –
MY INSPIRATIONAL JOURNEY TO SUCCESS

Published by
10-10-10 Publishing
1-9225 Leslie St.
Richmond Hill
Ontario, Canada
L4B 3H6

ISBN-13: 978-1523605866

Copyright © January 2016 by Kalpna Suthar
London, England, United Kingdom
www.nowneverjudgeabook.com
E: kalpnasuthar@nowneverjudgeabook.com

All Rights Reserved

No part of this book may be reproduced, copied, stored or transmitted in any form or by any means – graphic, electronic or mechanical, including photocopying, recording or information storage and retrieval systems without permission in writing from both the copyright owner and the publisher of this book. This book is not intended to give any legal, medical, and/or financial advice to the readers.

For information about special discounts for bulk purchases, please contact 10-10-10 Publishing at 1-888-504-6257

Printed in the United States of America

Contents

About Kalpna Suthar	vii
Foreword	ix
Acknowledgements	xi
Chapter 1: The Dark Side	1
Chapter 2: The Realisation	17
Chapter 3: Dealing with the Consequences	29
Chapter 4: Starting from Scratch	37
Chapter 5: Learning Curves	49
Chapter 6: Wanting More	57
Chapter 7: Brand New Me	65
Chapter 8: The Finale	83

Dedicated to my mother, father, brother and nan

About Kalpna Suthar

Kalpna Suthar lives in the East End of London, UK, where she was born and grew up. She graduated in LLB (Hons) Law and Criminology after her time at university and soon after joined the Metropolitan Police. After working for them for over six years she decided to change her career path, and worked in organising various events around London for the Mayor of London programme. She later was given the opportunity to work with the Liberal Democrat political party in 2015 during the London Election.

Her hobbies are Muay Thai, travelling, meeting people from all walks of life, and continuously learning ways of self-development in order to better herself and to help others.

Foreword

I am extremely impressed with Kalpna Suthar's high level of bravery, determination and strength.

After reading this powerful book, I recommend it as a must read! I feel this book should be mandatory for anyone who wants the push they need to motivate them to accomplish their goals, regardless of their current situation. What makes this book fascinating is that it explains that, no matter what you're going through, your mindset and positive thinking is the answer to freedom and achieving your goals.

Kalpna finally plucked up the courage to put pen to paper, sharing her past experiences, and has opened the eyes of many people who are going through similar phases in their life. Not only is it inspiring but she has shown commitment and dedication to changing everything around her into a positive.

In this book you will come to understand that each one of you, no matter your background, has the potential to change your life around, even when you believe that there is no getting out. No matter how hard you feel you have hit rock bottom, the power you hold within is far greater than you could possibly imagine.

Raymond Aaron
New York Times Best-selling Author

Acknowledgements

I want to thank Nazia Khatun for taking me on as her client and being my personal coach. She has taught me so much, from nutrition to positive thinking, and provided the first stepping stone to my own success.

I want to thank Tahmina Begum (AKA Tammy Bee) for identifying that I have the ability and skills to work in Events and for guiding me in the right direction. I thank you for all your support.

I want to thank Ginna Andrew and Desreen Corbett, the two people that I consider to be my oldest friends. Even though I haven't been around, they have always congratulated me in all my achievements and encouraged me to do my best.

I thank Claire Napper for being one of my closest friends and for being my inspiration in many ways, that even she has no knowledge about. I thank her for all those conversations we had about life, and for bringing great ideas my way.

I especially want to thank my mum, dad, brother and nan for all the continuous support that they have shown me, even when I haven't been around as much.

I want to thank Tony Robbins for being an inspiring role model. I have found that his teachings through his events have helped me to push and motivate myself.

Kalpna Suthar

I want to thank Dr Demartini as it was his 'Values' event that I attended in London that put many things in perspective for me.

I want to thank Rhonda Byrne for writing "The Secret," and her subsequent books. They have motivated and inspired me to keep on moving forward, even when times were hard. I believe that these books opened my eyes to greater opportunities.

I want to thank Raymond Aaron and his team for helping me edit, format, publish and market this book. Without their guidance I would have been lost.

I want to thank John Lee for his helpful tips on Facebook, and pushing to continuously inspire others.

I want to thank Tyrese Gibson and Dwayne Johnson for their motivating videos on YouTube and their inspirational quotes on social media.

I want to thank Tim Fisher and Jennifer Ward for believing in me, supporting me and pushing me to be the best that I can be. Finally I would like to thank Matt Lloyd, Russell Whitney and Kelly Doxtator for giving me the opportunity to meet Raymond Aaron. Without their support and trust in me I would not have managed to get my book started, let alone getting it completed.

Chapter 1
The Dark Side

Home/Family

Arrrggghhh . . . what is wrong with them . . . why do they hate me so much? What is wrong with her, she gets on my nerves! My mum has always hated me but my younger brother can do no wrong. She has always treated him better than me . . . she only criticizes and complains about me . . . but really, what does she expect?!

My brother was about 4 years old and I was 12. It was a weekend, a really cold day and raining. My mum was going round the corner to buy some milk and asked both me and my brother if we wanted anything. My brother loved Rollos and asked for a tube of them. I loved Curley Wurleys, a long funny shaped chocolate covered caramel thin stick. I was always really happy to be eating one of those . . . it was the best feeling. So my mum went out to get the milk and she came back with a bag, so my brother went running to get his Rollo and I went to get my chocolate. My brother ripped open the packet and gobbled them up in no time; you could see on his face that he was really content with stuffing his face. I looked in the bag and all I could find was milk. I asked my mum where my chocolate was and she replied "I didn't get it." When I asked why not she said "Because your brother told me not to get it for you."

My heart sank; I couldn't believe my mum would listen to a 4 year old kid. I was so upset I went crying . . . and told my dad, who then spoke to my mum. She did feel bad after and offered to go buy me my Curley Wurley, but it was too late. My mum already showed me that I was no good, that I wasn't anything to her. From then on I knew that this was what it would be like for the rest of my life . . . my mum would always choose my brother over me, and so naturally I rebelled and retaliated over everything little thing that happened. I wasn't wanted by my mother so why should I bother listening to her; why would I even respect her???

As I went into my adolescence my relationship with my mother went from bad to worse. I wanted to go out with my friends to a house party . . . it was a 16th birthday party and it was on the same road that I lived on. I was planning on going with my friend who lived opposite me. We decided what to wear and I was so excited . . . my first house party . . . woohoo!!! But when I asked my mum if could go and she said "no" I got really frustrated. So many of my friends were going; I had to be there. I asked my mum again but she continued to say no. I pleaded with her and I said "It's only at the top of the road!" At this point my mum and I were arguing and shouting and I told her that I was going whether she liked it or not. She started chasing me up the stairs and told me that I couldn't go; that she was the mother and I had to listen to her . . . "What a bloody hypocrite," I said to myself. "So she wants to be my mum when it suits her, but she is happy to choose my brother over me any time." I hit the roof. I told her that I was going whether she liked it or not, and she told me if I went I was not to come back. At this point I was so angry I didn't care.

I left the house and went to the party. I had the best time at the party but for about a week my mum did not speak to me and we both avoided each other. A couple of weeks later everything went back to normal. I didn't understand what was wrong with my mum . . . she was the one who decided that my brother was more important than me, and yet she continued to ask me what was wrong with me. I told her several times that she favoured my brother over me, but she always denied it; even when there was a pattern of favouritism, and I had given her several examples. For a long time when I was younger I resented my brother, and we would both quarrel all the time. Again my mum would side with my brother, and to be honest I did try to wind him up, but only because he was a little squirt.

As I grew older I realised that this wasn't my brother's fault at all, but rather it had everything to do with my mum. She was the adult; she was the one that was supposed to be wiser. I had so much resentment for my mum that I would flip out on her for any little thing. I couldn't do anything right by my mum anyway, so why the hell would I support or agree with anything she said? For many years my mum and I argued about everything. I hated her. I had no support from my family, not even from my dad; he always agreed with my mum, even if he knew she was wrong, just because he wanted to keep the peace. But there was no peace as far as I was concerned with me and my mum; she was public enemy number one, and I wasn't going to stand for it. If she wanted to fight, then I was going to give her one . . . and I was never going to back down. It was on!!!

"Darkness cannot drive out darkness; only light can do that. Hate cannot drive out hate; only love can do that."
Martin Luther King, Jr.

School

I used to love school and I always preferred to be at school than be at home any day of the week, but I hated getting up for school. It was a pain. All I wanted to do was stay under the covers and sleep, especially on those cold winters days, and let's face it, there's a lot of it in London.

A normal day in school for me consisted of a detention first thing in the morning, for being late the day before. Ironically I was usually late for detention. I then used to go and meet with my friends, who were awesome and the best people I have met. Many of them knew each other from primary school but I had attended a different primary school, and so I knew no one.

My favorite subjects were Art, IT and Physical Education, and I always excelled in these subjects. I had to be the best; if I wasn't then it just wasn't good enough for me. My least favorite subjects were Mathematics, History, Religious Education and Geography . . . sitting for an hour in these classes was hell! I was continuously looking at the clock waiting for it to be over. And, funny enough, I was always getting into trouble in these subjects, and it didn't help that my teachers were completely incompetent. My Maths teacher had such a strong African accent that we couldn't even understand what he was saying, and with our GCSE exams round the corner . . . it was really worrying. I remember one day I had forgotten my exercise book in my locker and asked if I could go and get it.

He said no, and when I asked him to suggest what I could write on, he gave me a sheet of paper, but it was already used and had writing on it. I lost it. I told him that my parents paid his wages through tax, and at that point my Maths teacher told me that I had detention during lunch the next day. That made me mad as we only had an hour for lunch and detention was for a whole 15 minutes. I told him that he should give me a fresh sheet of paper or allow me to go and get my book from my locker, but he was afraid that if he let me go then I wouldn't come back. To be honest I had done this before with a few of my friends. A few of us used to sneak out and hide behind the bushes to have a smoke. What's the point of sitting in a room watching a man pointing at the board and talking when we had no idea what he was saying?

Never Judge a Book by its Cover

At that moment I found it funny how adults hate being told they are wrong by a teenager and found them to be such hypocrites and these are the people in our lives who are meant to teach us from right and wrong, and who we are supposed to look up to . . . this was a complete joke!

Whilst in my Maths class my PE (Physical Education) teacher pulled me out of my class as she wanted to speak to me. She was a mean woman and was built like a man. In fact she looked like a huge boulder . . . a real scary looking woman. She told me that a student had complained about me and how I threatened to beat her up and as a result she was found crying in the corridor. I had no idea what she was talking about.

She asked again, "Did you yell at someone in the corridor and threaten to beat them up?" I told her no! She looked surprised that I had no recollection of this but . . . honestly . . . I had not threatened to beat anyone up or yell at them in the corridor.

The next day I had my PE lesson and she pulled one of my peers out of the class and spoke to her outside and then later sent her in and asked to speak to me outside. My teacher once again asked if I had had some sort of altercation with the girl she pulled out earlier in my class, and I once again told her no, and she sent me back into the classroom.

My friends were asking me what was going on; I told them and they knew exactly what was going on and just smiled. As I walked back into the classroom my teacher asked to speak to this other girl again and it was only a few minutes that she asked to speak to me again as well, so now this other girl, my teacher and I were outside. My teacher told me that she was found in the corridor crying as I had yelled at her and threatened to beat her up. I turned around and said, "First of all I did not yell at her and secondly I did not threaten to beat her up." I then went on to say "But she needs a slap ."

My teacher hit the roof for wasting her time. I told her that she needed to get her facts right before she started accusing people. She started yelling and calling me a bully, and telling me that I thought I was smart. I told her, "Well clearly I'm smarter than you." At this point she told me that I had detention at lunch that day . . . I told her that I couldn't make it as I already had detention with my maths teacher, from the day before. Well she just loved that . . . honestly I thought it was hilarious.

What had happened with this girl was in my Science lesson she had been shouting the odds to the teacher and as a result the whole class ended up getting detention during lunch, and when I saw her later that day in the corridor I pointed at her and said "You need a slap" and apparently she must have walked away crying and was found by my PE teacher . . . just my flaming luck.

> *"Education is the most powerful weapon which you can use to change the world."*
> Nelson Mandela

College

College was completely different than high school. I mean my school was an all-girl school and . . . well in college . . . there were boys everywhere . . . I also had one sit next to me in a few of my classes. I had no idea didn't know how to talk to boys. There was a time when there was a boy sitting next to me in class and I felt so awkward that I looked at him thinking "Why the hell is he sitting here, find somewhere else."

My first reaction to boys was to be defensive and to attack. This boy asked me for a pen and that was it . . . I annoyingly asked him "Why would you come to college without a pen?" and then handed him a pen which I didn't get back.

Five months went by and I softened up to the boys and was able to make friends and talk to them like all my female friends . . . well, not exactly like my female friends ... they never appreciated me talking to them about makeup or shopping! I soon met a boy in college and we became friends, and then started a relationship.

This was my first relationship and I had no idea how to be a girlfriend. We arranged our first date one Saturday . . . I was looking forward to it and decided what I would wear, how I would do my hair and makeup in a week in advance. We decided where our meeting point was and I got the bus that very day and met him at the agreed time. I had arrived on time, and waited and waited. I called him and he said that he was running late, so again I waited and waited. I was getting so annoyed and frustrated and thought about going home a few times. It was cold and raining and I was waiting at a bus stop.

An hour had passed and I decided that when the next bus arrived I would get on and go home. I could see the bus approaching from the distance and got ready to get on, but as I looked around I saw him walking up towards me. I decided not to get on the bus but I was so angry I actually started yelling at him, and that was how the relationship began!

We used to see each other almost every day, during break and lunch and then after class. We spoke to each other on the phone every evening on the phone, once we both got home. We could spend hours on the phone talking about anything and everything.

So as our relationship grew we were inseparable; everyone at college knew we were together. A lot of people didn't approve, and there were a few boys who even approached him and told him that they had their eye on me, and he replied "Yeah, you used to." Everyone saw us together at college all the time and knew that we were a couple; if I was around it was guaranteed that he wouldn't be far behind, and vice versa.

Soon things started to change and it got very scary . . . we were constantly arguing about everything . . . I couldn't do anything right! This felt like my relationship with my mum all over again. I felt as though anything I said would set him off . . . and I started to realise that he had a huge temper. At this point I knew what his mum meant when she asked me if I thought I could handle his temper. When she asked me this which was at the very beginning stages of us dating, I looked at her surprised and didn't know what she was talking about, he was really sweet and kind, "he doesn't have a temper," I said. How wrong was I!

I later found that my boyfriend was involved in a lot of things he shouldn't have been involved in; a lot of it involved weapons and he showed me the secret place in his room where he kept them hidden. I remember one day I was running late and was rushing to get to my English class on time. I opened the door and looked at my teacher and apologised for being late. I then sat next to my friends Nina and Joseph. On this day we were talking about Shakespeare and his plays . . . we were all trying to read Beowulf but as they are in old Shakespearean language we were having difficulties translating them. Somehow I realised that in fact I was really good at reading and understanding Shakespeare and I helped my classmates.

A few of us, including Joseph, stayed behind. He asked for my help, and as I leaned over to read what he was referring to and then, he kissed me. I pulled back straight away and looked at him in shock. I quickly got all my stuff together and left the room. Nina came after me and asked what happened, and I told her. She looked at me with wide eyes and asked if I was going to tell my boyfriend. We both knew that he was going to freak out. I told Nina I had to tell him; I'd rather him find out through me than from someone else.

I was right; the minute I told him he got mad and asked where he kissed me. I pointed to my lips and he stormed off, pushing past his friends. They looked at me and asked what was going on; I told them "Just make sure he doesn't do anything stupid." I called him on his phone constantly, but he wouldn't picked up. I was so worried; I knew his temper would get the better of him and he would behave in a crazy manner where he would be capable of anything.

During the afternoon break I went to the canteen with my friends and I saw him there. I went to talk to him and he told me not to touch him. I looked at him and asked why not, and he told me to keep away from him. I told him I didn't do anything wrong. Then he pulled up his t-shirt and showed me what he had with him . . . I asked him, "What the hell are you going to do with that?" He asked "Where is he?" but I didn't know. He went looking for him with his friends, and my friends and I went after them, They found Joseph outside at the bus stop. As soon as my boyfriend saw him he pulled it out and pointed it at him. Months went by and I remember a day where I was walking from college to the bus station and I was jumped by a group of men. I have found out later that my boyfriend had gotten into some sort of altercation with them previously. Well . . . today was the scariest day . . . the group of men decided to follow me down a high street. It was a busy street with lots of people around, but then it happened . . . all of a sudden I felt a huge thud on my back and I went flying on the ground.

One of the men had taken a running kick and went for my back. I fell to the floor hard and all I felt were kicks on my head, back, and belly. I didn't know what was going on. I was trying to protect myself by shielding my face and my belly with my arms and by curling inwards but I was getting kicked everywhere.

The next minute, I heard running footsteps. They were getting closer, and then the kicking stopped and I could hear men shouting. I was helped up and taken into an Estate Agent shop that was just across the road. A group of men who were working in the shop had seen what was happening and ran out to my rescue. My lip was bleeding, and I had bruises on my face as well as on my body. I was aching all over. I cried, and the first thought that came to mind was how can I go home to my parents like this.

Friends

A lot of my friends from school decided to attend the same college as I did. Although we all chose to study different subjects . . . the gang was back! We hung out all the time. We met each other in the college canteen during breaks, and decided where we would go for lunch. We also got a few shopping sprees in now and again.

A few friends from our school decided to attend other colleges, and we arranged to meet up with them for a catch up once in a while. I was a sociable type and made many friends in college. I introduced a lot of them to my friends from school, and we all became a huge group of friends.

I became friends with a group of girls who were Jamaican and called themselves 'Yardy.' You didn't want to mess with these girls or make them mad; they were capable of anything, and they fought better than men!

Many of my friends had boyfriends from the same group of male friends. I was the dependable friend that they came to lean on when things were going terribly wrong with their boyfriends, and I was the one that gave them words of advice. Whenever they called or wanted to meet up you could guarantee that I would be there. I really didn't have a problem with this; you see, loyalty is a big thing for me and I was super loyal to my friends. But I was about to learn a lesson . . .

There was a boy in college who sparked my interest, and eventually we became a couple which meant a lot of my time was taken up with him. My friends didn't like him and they had no problem telling me. All of a sudden when my friends called I wasn't able to drop everything and come and meet them. I missed their phone calls. I had a boyfriend and they were not happy. Apparently I was being a really bad friend and had no time for them anymore. I was fuming for years. I was there for them, especially when they had boyfriend issues, and the first relationship I got involved in and they didn't like it. Why couldn't they be there for me this time?

It was clear that they had all been talking behind my back. Nina was the one who was leading the pack. Yes, the one I knew from school; she had been talking to all my other friends and now they had all turned on me. I was devastated, especially as they all knew each other through me. The distrust, betrayal and loyalty all went out the window, and my heart sank. We were no longer friends and we all went our separate ways.

I decided to do what I had to do and get my head down and get my qualification from college. If they wanted to talk to me they knew where I was, but we ignored each other in the corridors, and during breaks in the canteen we acted like we didn't know each other it was pretty sad of what these friendships had become. Even when we caught each other's eyes we looked the other way. It was clear that we were no longer friends!

Nina's birthday was coming up and I wondered if I should at least text her happy birthday, but we hadn't spoken to each other for months. I decided not to text her, and one afternoon when my classes had finished for the day I went to the bus stop outside of the college to travel home. Nina and a few of my other friends . . . or should I say ex-friends . . . arrived soon after. They all saw me there as I was the only one at this bus stop and pretty hard to miss. They were talking amongst themselves and Nina thanked them for her birthday surprise and presents.

There was another girl with them; a girl that I never saw hang out with them before. She came up to me and asked why I didn't turn up to the surprise party. She was very sincere and I could tell that she was unaware of what had happened to our friendship, so I replied "Because I had no idea and was not invited."

I could see the stunned look on her face and at that moment my bus arrived and I got on. It was at that moment that I realised that there was no way that our friendship could ever go back to what it was . . . not as long as I was still with my boyfriend . . . but why should I have to choose? That isn't what it means to be a friend; they should have been supporting me no matter what, just like I did for them for years.

> "What I have found is that real friends stand by you."
> Jeffrey Archer

University

Sitting in front of my PC at college, I had no idea what I wanted to study in university. I literally had a list of courses up on my screen and closed my eyes, pointed at the screen while it scrolled down, and then I landed my finger on the screen and stopped scrolling. The subject that my finger landed on was the course I would study. I opened my eyes and it was Law and Criminology.

Three months in and I discovered that I hated university and thought about dropping out; the only things I liked were the new friends I made. I felt a sense of relief; I had no baggage or anyone that knew me here, I was able to start all over. It was my new friends at university that kept me going. They told me to give it a chance; it had only been 3 months and it was only the beginning stages.

So I stayed and I found myself in the university library quite often, we decided to have study groups when exams were approaching. I was still with my boyfriend at this point but things were going downhill very fast. I didn't want to believe it, but it started to affect my studies. He was a very insecure person, and often asked if I was seeing someone else and meeting them in the library. No matter how many times I told him no, he still insisted and made comments about my "other boyfriend."

He started telling me that I was not allowed to cut or colour my hair, that I wasn't able to eat certain foods, and I was to eat what he had offered even if I didn't want it. My hair was jet black and wavy, and came down to my waist. So naturally I retaliated against these rules; I walked into my usual hair salon and told them that I want a hair cut. When they asked how much, I was so angry at my boyfriend that I told them to cut it all off.

They looked at me in shock. I described how I wanted my hair cut, basically it was a graduated bob shaved at the back -- and I told them that I wanted to dye my hair with blocks of royal blue and peacock green, with my fringe being blue. The hairdressers were excited! This was completely crazy and they loved doing unusual styles, and took it on as a challenge.

I saw my boyfriend that evening and, yes you can guessed it, we got into yet another argument. He was angry because I disobeyed him, and asked me what his family were to think. I told him that I liked it and that there was no way he could tell me what to do. That evening he got physical again but this time he didn't leave any marks.

The next day I was late for my lecture at university. As I opened the door everyone in the theatre room looked at me as I walked up the stairs; they were surprised but all said that they liked my hair and it suited me. I got had to admit it was a dramatic change, but that was the point!

My relationship with my boyfriend got really bad, and I was no longer able to concentrate on my studies. This was showing in my results; there was no talking to him anymore. If I said anything he got mad, if I didn't say anything he got mad. One way or another I had a beating to look forward to.

I became withdrawn and quiet. I didn't know what to do anymore. I wasn't happy and I didn't know what to do to make things better. My studies were now being affected and I had to re-take many of my modules. I was embarrassed by this. My friends were passing their course with flying colours and I was failing. "They probably think that I'm stupid," I thought to myself. Maybe my boyfriend was right. I could no longer let my head round the materials I was reading for my course; I was researching, reading journals, going to the library, but nothing would stick. I couldn't remember anything, even with the hundreds of post-it notes I had to remind me all over my text books and my bedroom wall. My mind seemed to be elsewhere and I just couldn't shake it off.

Chapter 2
The Realisation

Frightened

As time went on I can remember that his temper got worsened and he started to get physical more often, kicking at my ribs, bleeding lips, I was constantly crying in this relationship . . . I was frightened! I didn't want to be a punching bag any more, but I didn't know how to get out?

It had been almost 5 years in this relationship, and even though he was never like this in the beginning, he became more and more aggressive. He used to tell me that it was me who made him so angry, but I didn't know what I was doing wrong.

I got to a point that I didn't know what to say when we argued. I always knew where it was leading to, and that no matter what I said he was coming for me. I was always wrong. If I said anything he told me not to talk back, if I kept my mouth shut he yelled and told me to talk. He constantly told me I was fat and ugly that no one else would want me.

When someone you consider to love you continuously tells you the same thing, you automatically start thinking it's true, which is what happened to me. I thought I was better off staying with him because no one else would want me? Is this what love meant? How can he tell me he loves me and then make me feel this way?

I lost my confidence in every aspect of my life, I started to question everything: things I spoke to people about at university, how I spoke to them . . . . they must think I'm stupid too . . . maybe I should keep my mouth shut all the times.

My boyfriend told me not to tell anyone about what he used to do to me; his eyes always looked so evil when he told me that I knew if I did tell anyone the next time it would be worse. When he got angry, I always got up and defended myself because that is what the people say to do, right? That the bully will leave you alone once you stand up for yourself. But it was almost like this gave him more reason to keep shouting and hitting me.

There was a time when we were in the car and he was driving; I was sitting in the passenger seat. I can't even remember what we were talking about, but he got angry again. I became a pro at identifying his stages of anger: first he started to question what I was saying, and if I didn't give the answer he wanted his voice started raising, and he repeated the same questions again . . . "Is that what you're saying?" "Tell me; I want you to tell me."

As he started yelling, I was scared that he was going to lose control of the car and we would get into an accident. My heart started beating and I was shouting "Stop the car, pull over and we can talk," but he kept on driving. In fact he started speeding and revving the engine, which frightened me even more. He kept shouting at me "What is wrong with you? You always make me angry. This is all your fault." He had that look on his face . . . I had seen it many times before. His eyes tightened like his jaw and he had that vein on his forehead that was pulsating. He started to clench his hands to a fist and then it happened . . . his left fist came flying towards my face . . . my nose and lip started bleeding.

I started crying and he started to get even more angry because I was hurt and crying. We eventually got to his house where his parents, older brother and younger sister lived. He told me "You better fix your face before my family sees you." So I wiped the tears and blood from my face, walked into his house and said hello to his family like everything was ok.

I could see that his mother noticed that something was wrong from my face, that something wasn't right, but she never said anything and acted completely normal. He went storming upstairs to his room and shut the door, and I stayed downstairs with his family for a while. To be honest I was waiting for him to cool off before I went to speak to him again.

I gave him about 20 minutes . . . you see if I left it too long I knew this would also make him angry. I went up in his room and he was in bed with the covers over him. I asked him if he was ok and he turned round and lifted the covers to let me lie next to him. He asked me why I did this to him, why I made him so angry. I told him I didn't know and I apologised to him.

I was apologising a lot in this relationship . . . it was always because of me that he got angry and I had reached a point where I thought that I deserved to be beaten . . . I was the one that made him angry. The way I made a cup of tea, leaving the tea bag inside, made him angry too, and told me that I couldn't do anything right.

He asked me to make pasta for him one day, and after adding pasta to the pan I poured hot water over it and then put it on the cooker to boil. He got mad at me for doing this as well . . . he told me "Who taught you to put hot water? It needs to be cold water." But did it really matter? Apparently it did; I was kicked in the ribs for it that evening.

Kalpna Suthar

"Anybody can become angry - that is easy, but to be angry with the right person and to the right degree and at the right time and for the right purpose, and in the right way - that is not within everybody's power and is not easy."
Aristotle

Depression

I hated my family, I had no friends, my boyfriend was a psycho and I didn't even love him any more. I felt alone and had no one to turn to. I didn't trust the people that were around me and had no one to vent to . . . I had to keep it all inside and solve it myself. All I seemed to do was cry every night, and I hated my life and myself. I always questioned why this was happening to me . . . what I had done that was so wrong.

I wasn't sleeping or eating but somehow I was still putting on a ton of weight. Most nights I went to sleep crying . . . I was pathetic and helpless, there was no hope for me! I didn't want to do anything, I wanted to be left alone. My family were irritating me when I was around them; every time my mum spoke it irritated me. I didn't want to be around my boyfriend either.

I was tired all the time, physically, mentally and emotionally. I wanted to stay in bed all day in my pyjamas and not talk to anyone. When my mum came into my room to see how I was doing as she didn't see me all day, I would get mad at her for interrupting me and yell at her, asking her to leave me alone and to leave my room. She would start to yell back and tell me that this was her house and she could come and go as she pleased. This made me even more angry! I couldn't speak to my family about it, all they would have done was tell me "I told you so," especially as they had no idea about this relationship I was in. . . . all I had was me, myself and I.

From the beginning my parents told me he was a bad apple but I paid no notice, and I continued in the relationship even after they told me not to. So for 5 years I was in a relationship that they had no idea about. I started to feel more and more depressed. Any little task seemed so hard and so much effort, and I couldn't control all the negative thoughts, no matter how much I tried. I was irritable, short-tempered and more aggressive than usual; my mum even told me that I needed to do something about my temper. I didn't have a temper; I was angry because she was making me angry and she always knew which buttons to press. Hold on . . . does this remind you of someone, I sound like my boyfriend now!!! Anything she said, even her just opening her mouth, mad me angry.

I was engaging in more reckless behaviour . . . I couldn't concentrate on anything else. I tried to pass my driving test but had failed 6 times already. I was getting really low marks at university and on some occasions I had to re-do the whole assignment or exam.

Even my nan was on my case, telling me that I needed to learn to drive and that I hadn't passed my test yet. My parents had spent a lot of money on my lessons and my nan reminded me constantly of this. But I couldn't tell anyone what was going on, what I was going through; I had to keep it all inside, and the only release I had was to get angry at people or cry. I had built up so much anger and I just kept seeing red. I could always feel when I got angry and it lay in the pit of my stomach; it was like a round ball and as I got angrier, this ball got bigger and bigger. I couldn't think straight about anything. I felt like the whole world was out to get me and I had to keep fighting everyone. I told my boyfriend that he couldn't carry on treating me like this every time he got mad, and it got to the point that when anyone got him angry he took it out on me. I told him several times that if he carried on then I would leave, that I was holding on to a piece of thread and didn't know how much longer I could hold on. He looked at me seriously for a moment and then turned round and said "You won't leave me; you need me." He was really cocky about it. I didn't bother wasting my breath explaining to him that I would leave; I didn't have the energy and I didn't want to fight any more.

Suicidal

I didn't want to live anymore; I wanted the crying and hurt to stop! I thought about hurting myself all the time but I never had the guts to cut myself. I wanted to . . . I deserved it . . . "I'm a horrible person, girlfriend and daughter," I told myself.

I thought about cutting my wrists or overdosing on pills with alcohol, again and again, but I didn't have the courage. "What is wrong with me? I can't even do this . . . I'm so pathetic. People would be better off without me, they would all have a much better life. How do I make things right?"

I hoped and prayed, almost every night, that I would die in my sleep or get run over by a truck. I didn't even trust myself anymore, with the thoughts that were going in my head . . . they were things I didn't think I was ever capable of but maybe I was???

I didn't know what was going on with me. I was so angry all the time; I thought about hurting people, my family or just random people that I passed on the street that I found to be rude . . . I would just want to turn round and throw a punch at everyone that came in my way. I couldn't sleep and kept waking up several times during the night, and for this reason I was always tired and had no energy. I stopped taking care of myself; I didn't see much point of it anymore.

I was smoking a lot more and drinking alcohol constantly; this is what my life consisted of. I would drink with my boyfriend, with his friends whenever we met up, whether it be at someone's house, on the street corner, a house party, clubbing . . . it always consisted of the same thing. Even though I threw up many times and the very next day I would have a pounding headache I would still go out that evening and do it all over again. It was the only way I could forget about the hurt; it was the only time that I felt that I had control. As wrong as this may sound, it was the only time I actually got a glimpse of happiness. He had threatened me so many times, that he would leave me, that he wouldn't have any problems finding someone else, and that I needed him more than he needed me. And I was so fragile I believed it. I couldn't live without him; what was I going to do? I was scared. I relied on him so much, he was the only one I spoke to because no one else wanted to speak to me or be my friend. "He's right," I thought. "I am pathetic."

The summer arrived and I was on break. I managed to find a job for a couple of months as a switchboard operator/administrator, which was about 30 minute walk from my house. One morning I walked to work and popped into supermarket on the way to pick up my lunch for the day.

As I approached the junction to cross the street, I saw that the green man was lit on the pedestrian crossing, stating that pedestrians could cross. As I did, a red truck approached me. "It will stop when it gets closer," I thought to myself, but it was driving down at speed. I remember my carrier bag flying up in the air above me and everything coming out of the bag and falling towards me . . . it was a hit and run. There were pedestrians on the other side of the road that saw this and came running to see if I was ok; I was disorientated for a while, then I sat up and shook that feeling off.

At the time I didn't quite realise what had just happened. I remember people talking in horrified voices, I could hear them saying "and he just drove off", and then a male voice asked me if I was ok. I replied "yeah" and I could hear several voices saying "We need to call an ambulance." A few hands reached out and I grabbed one and stood up. People were still asking me if I was ok, and I said I was fine.

I brushed myself off and said thank you to the people who helped, and I continued to cross the road and went to work as normal. They were stunned and watched me walk away as though nothing had happened. The surprising thing was I didn't get a scratch on me, not even a bruise. You would never have thought I was in an accident, and in fact none of my colleagues even noticed. But then this got me thinking . . . I've asked to be knocked down by a truck so many times, was this the universe's way of giving me what I asked for? If it was, then the universe was playing a complete joke on me . . . I asked so my life would end, but I didn't even get a scratch on me . . . why not? Anyone else would have been dead . . . I was always the unlucky one!

I'm Done!

"I want more . . . this can't be what life is all about . . . there has to be something better out there." I knew I had put on weight and I wasn't happy with it so I started to go to the gym once a week with my mum, every Saturday, and then we would go to have a sauna at our local Leisure Centre. I told my boyfriend that I felt that I needed to do this, and he accepted it at the time. But as time went by he started to call me while I was at the gym and asked me to come and see him. I told him I was at the gym and I would come and see him later . . . because he didn't get his way, he started to get angry again and said "You're only going because of the men at the gym; you're flirting with them."

I told him I was not, and that I was going to the gym because I needed to lose weight, but he was adamant. To be honest I was avoiding men . . . I felt so fat and ugly that I lost all confidence and I no longer had the courage to speak to another man. One day after the gym, I decided to get my nails done. I had never had my nails done before and was really excited. I had been looking forward to it for days. I received a call from him; he asked me what I was doing, and I told him "I've just finished at the gym and on my way to the nail salon." He told me he missed me and wanted to see me. I said he would be seeing me a little later, and he said "I want to see you now."

Again I told him I was going to get my nails done. He completely flipped out. "Who are you doing your nails for? Someone at the gym? You didn't go to get your nails done before."

I told him that I was going because I wanted to get my nails done, as I'd never done it before. I told him I was doing it for me. This was my very first taste of wanting to take care of me in a long while and wanting to experience things that normal people did, even if it was as small as going for a manicure. He told me that he wanted to see me and I told him "later." He hated not getting his way, and he gave me an ultimatum . . . "You come and see me now or it's over."

I told him "Fine, then it's over."

"What the f***," he replied. "You're seeing someone else aren't you?"

"No," I said, "but I'm going to get my nails done. I'll talk to you later."

"No you won't; it's over."

"Ok fine, if that's what you want. I have to go." I put the phone down . . . I was really proud of myself for standing up to him . . . but I knew I was going to pay for that later. But I really didn't care. "I'm done with this!" I said to myself.

He was fuming at this stage and I could tell as he kept blowing up my phone with texts and calls, but I was no longer going to take this kind of treatment from him. "I was only going to get my nails done and this is how he reacts . . . what is the matter with him?"

I told him "I'm going, bye," and hung up the phone. He kept calling my phone and when I didn't answer I started getting abusive text messages from him. I didn't realise that my phone was on silent whilst I was getting my nails done. But when I left, I checked my phone and saw that I had 37 missed calls and 8 text messages. I didn't bother replying. I felt so good about myself; I had stood up for myself and no longer cared about him and besides I was too busy admiring my nails, they looked good. At the time I wasn't physically with him so he couldn't hurt me, and I felt a sense of release. When he told me that it was over, I didn't care . . . I didn't want to be in this relationship anymore and was quite happy to end it. I wasn't going to fight him or persuade him to take me back, not like I had done before.

"It's not what happens to you, but how you react to it that matters."
Epictetus

Dead or Alive

He told me that he would not let me go . . . if he couldn't have me then no one could. I told him, "Either way, whether you let me go or kill me, I will no longer be with you." That's when he looked at me stunned. You see in the past, every time he got angry and physical. I would get back up from the floor and fight back every time. I learnt that he used to get off on that, and kept pounding at me; I realised that he liked to see me get back up and try to fight him in order to defend myself, so he could knock me back down. But now what had changed was that I felt defeated and no longer had any fight left in me to get back up if he knocked me down.

I didn't care if he ended my life anymore; maybe just staying on the floor when he knocked me down was the best option. I would have preferred that my life had ended that to being with him any longer. I didn't want to live anymore. I wanted to feel happy but I had felt so depressed and frightened for so long that I had forgotten what it felt like to be happy. I felt like I had lost everything and had nothing to give. I had given everything in this relationship and had reached the end of my tether.

As he wasn't able to get through to me on the phone, he often waited for me in his car outside my house, so if I left my house he could speak to him. During lunch whilst I was at work and went to get my nails done, he was parked up on the high street. As I walked out I heard my name, so I looked round and saw him. He apologised over and over again, but I didn't want to listen to his apologies. They no longer meant anything to me; they were just words, as he had apologised several times before and still carried on every time he got angry.

I don't know what came over me; I only had an hour for lunch and he was cutting into my time and I really wasn't bothered to talk to him. He wasn't priority at that moment, so I told him "Dead or alive, either way, I'm not coming back to you . . . so do your worst . . . I'm done!"

He was shocked and stepped out of the car and said, "You're serious."

"Like a heart attack," I replied. "It's not like you haven't raised your hands on me before; you're actually quite experienced now, so what's stopping you?"

He stepped away from me and shook his head. He looked at me and said, "You actually mean it."

"Of course I do," I replied. "Why the hell do you want to be with me anyway? I'm fat and ugly; isn't that what you told me? Why are you so bothered that I don't want to be with you anymore?"

He didn't know what to say as he knew that this was the truth and couldn't believe I was saying it to him. I told him "I'm on lunch and have to get back," and walked away. He was calling for me but I carried on walking and continued with my day. As I walked away I couldn't believe what I had just done. A huge weight was lifted from my shoulders and I was smiling to myself on the inside.

"Once we accept our limits, we go beyond them."
Albert Einstein

Chapter 3
Dealing with the Consequences

Moving Out

He called me and told me he wanted all the gifts that he had ever given me back, and to put it all in a black bag and to leave it outside my front door for him to collect. I did exactly that. My family still had no idea what was going on and as I was upstairs looking out the window to keep an eye out for him they were all downstairs watching TV. I saw him pull up in his car. He parked across the street from me and walked across the road and into my front garden, but instead of collecting the bag he was hovering. I couldn't see exactly what he was doing . . . but then I realised he had an aerosol can and a lighter in his hands. He was lighting the bag on fire outside my door, where it could have burnt the whole of my house with my family inside. I went running down screaming "Someone is lighting a fire outside our door!"

By this time he had got into his car and driven off. My family came running out and we all saw the black bag on fire. My mum and my brother went in to get buckets of water to put on the fire; my dad was looking around and asking me "Who did this? Who have you gotten involved with, and gotten into their bad books?" As my brother and mum threw the water over the fire, we then cleared all the burnt debris into the bin, I saw him again. He drove back round and slowed down as he passed my house again, grinning. It was an evil grin and showed no remorse for what he had just done.

I could no longer hide this from my family; there was no way after this. I told them everything and my dad decided that it wasn't safe for us to stay there in our home for a while. "Next time," he said, "he could put something through the letterbox while we're asleep." And so we went to my Nan's house and stayed there for a few nights. I changed my number so that he could no longer contact me. His sister and mother had tried to call me as well, but I didn't want to talk to anyone who was associated with him.

They're his family," I said to myself. "Of course they will side with him."

My Nan was surprised to see us all, especially with some of our clothes with us. My mum explained to my Nan what had happened. I was so embarrassed. My Nan set up some sheets on the floor for us to sleep on. My parents were angry and disappointed, and I could tell this by the looks on their faces. I had let them down big time! My Nan was very calm and supportive. My parents and brother moved back home after a few days, but they still didn't think it was safe for me to move back, so for a few months it was me and my Nan.

They called me on my Nan's phone and visited me after work and on the weekend. They didn't completely forget about me, and checked on me quite frequently. I got to the point where I didn't want to eat, drink and couldn't sleep. I didn't want to talk to anyone and stayed indoors for over a week. My Nan used to cook and bring me food to eat but to be honest I was never hungry and completely lost my appetite. I wanted to be left alone and was definitely not up for a conversation.

My Nan wasn't a very forceful woman, but rather gentle. She gave me a week and then used her art of persuasion to get me out into the real world . . . guilt! She turned round and told me that there was no food in the house and that she needed my help to carry the shopping . . . and it worked. I felt so guilty, especially after all that she had done. As soon as I stepped out my eyes felt sensitive to the sunlight and took a while to adjust. We went to the supermarkets, but I felt so lost and out of place. I kept looking around thinking "He's going to pop up from nowhere," and I really didn't want to see him . . . plus I knew if my nan got her hands on him, he wouldn't have a chance. My nan was lethal with that handbag of hers!

Good Riddance

He was very persistent. Two months had passed and he was still parking up on the streets trying to catch me so he could speak to me. .He kept apologising and telling me that he could change, and to give him one more chance. I told him, "I have told you for months that I was just holding on but you never took me seriously. Instead you told me that I could never leave you, that I needed you . . . really? Is this what you still think? You push a person far enough and they will react; there is only so much a person can take, and now I have nothing left to give. I don't want to be in this relationship, and you need to leave me alone."

He asked me if I had changed my number as he had been trying to call but couldn't get through I told him "Of course I have; doesn't that tell you anything? Maybe that I don't want to speak to you anymore?"

I couldn't believe what happened next . . . he started crying. "Really???" I thought to myself, "Is that really meant to change my mind about everything, especially after all the nights I went to sleep crying and all the times I ended up crying because he had raised his hand on me?" He then started begging, begging me to come back to him. But now I feared going back to him, and whilst I had him out of my hair for a couple months now, it felt so good. At that moment I was so mad at him and at the same time looked at him and he was so pathetic. He would do anything to get his way and would stoop so low. One lunch time I walked out of the nail salon after getting a manicure and pedicure. He was in his car parked up. I didn't see him at first, as I was way too busy admiring my nails. Then I heard someone shout out my name; I looked up and it was him. He waved me over and as I passed he told me that he should have gotten me pregnant; that way I would never have been able to leave him.

"What makes you think I would have kept it?" I asked.

"Because I wouldn't have let you get rid of it," he replied.

I turned and said to him, "That is the exact reason why I wouldn't have told you."

He looked at me, shocked. "You would never have said that to me five years ago."

I told him "And you never had raised your hands on me five years ago!"

He told me that he would agree to go counselling. You see, several times in the past I had suggested that he go to counselling, but he always told me that he didn't need it, that it was always me that made him angry. But now he was telling me he would do whatever was necessary to get me back.

"This is a complete joke," I said. "Why didn't you think about this before? Now it's too late. I'm not with you and will not be coming back to you regardless . . . it makes no difference what you do now as it's over and you don't concern me anymore!"

He couldn't believe what I was saying. He kept telling me that he understood, and that he was sorry, but I knew this was just another tactic and if he agreed with everything I said I might just be fooled and get back together with him. But what he didn't realise was that I knew him really well and knew his games. I knew him more than he knew me; clearly he had paid no attention in this relationship. And if he actually thought I would never leave after this kind of treatment, that itself showed that he didn't know me. In fact, he soon learnt that he actually needed me more than I needed him.

"Forgive your enemies, but never forget their names."
John F. Kennedy

Hurting My Family

My family felt betrayed. I had kept this relationship a secret for five years, and although they had a feeling that something wasn't right, I denied it every time they asked me. I couldn't bring myself to tell them. I didn't know what to do to make it up to them . . . all I could say was sorry! But that didn't compete with what I had done . . . how could I fix this? "They will never trust me again, they hate me . . . they won't want me back . . . and I don't blame them, I am an awful daughter. They warned me that he was a bad apple, but I didn't listen . . . how could they see this but I couldn't?" I had so many questions going through my head. I decided that I was really going to work hard to earn their trust back, and I was never going to doubt them again. If I had listened to them before, I wouldn't have gone through what I did.

They were still worried about my safety. They would often see him parked outside the house, waiting for me to come out. My family thought it was best if I stayed round my Nan's house a bit longer. He never came to the house or approached my parents or my brother; he just sat and waited in the car. I can't imagine how my parents were feeling.

My mum asked me if he ever hurt me and after all of this, how could I have told her that he did? No parent wants to hear that their child was ever hurt by anyone. This would devastate them even more. I couldn't bear hurting them again, so I told my mum no. I felt ashamed and embarrassed. I really didn't know what was going through my family's minds at that moment. "What can they be thinking of me?" I wondered. "But ... my mum never cared about me; that's why she always favoured my brother. But she is being so supportive now . . . and all those times I was so horrible to her . . . I felt so bad! I never felt that she was ever there for me before, but now . . . well she's here now, at a point where I need her the most. They are all here for me. I hope they forgive me. There is that saying 'forget and forgive' but I'm sure this is not something that any of us will ever be able to forget. Does that mean that they will never forgive me?"

> "Mistakes are always forgivable,
> if one has the courage to admit them."
> Bruce Lee

Feeling Isolated/ A Failure

I was all on my own and even though my Nan, parents and brother phone or came to see me often, I still felt like I was on this planet on my own. There was no one that I could really talk to . . . no one who would understand me. I had fallen in a huge hole and didn't know how to get out.

"Everybody thinks I'm totally stupid; no one would even want to bother with me." The negative thoughts kept swirling through my mind. But my Nan had a way to make it all better. She used to sit with me and talk to me . . . all I really had to do was listen. She told me that I messed up, but now I needed to get back on my feet and try to do the right thing.

Every night before she went to bed, she brought me a shot of brandy and told me to drink it. "It will strengthen you and grow hairs on your chest," she said. She did this for about a week. My Nan was the only one I could talk to; she was really the only person constantly around me. My Nan never overwhelmed me and gave me my space, but at the same time she pushed me to get back to myself again. Although it did take some time, she never gave up on me . . . I am very grateful for this!

My nan's favorite programme on TV was Deal or No Deal. Every day without fail she would watch this. At the time I had no idea it was her favorite. She knew the exact times and channels, and every day on the dot she would come into the living room and switch the channel over . . . at the beginning I used to think to myself "No, not this again," but after a while I got into it as well. Whenever I left the house my nan always came with me. It was almost as if my Nan was my security guard. But I didn't complain or argue about it, as I knew she only had my best interest at heart.

In this life, we have to make many choices. Some are very important choices. Some are not. Many of our choices are between good and evil. The choices we make, however, determine to a large extent our happiness or our unhappiness, because we have to live with the consequences of our choices'. James E. Faust

"I am such a failure." I had wasted five years of my life and have nothing to show for it. How did this happen? How did I get this low? I kept failing my driving test and just got through my exams in university. I didn't have a job lined up; I kept applying for jobs and going to interviews but was never successful. I was so annoyed and disappointed with myself. I knew I had to take care of myself and work on myself. He had left me so distraught that I didn't know who I was. For a while I thought about leaving my family and going to a place where no one knew me so I could work on myself.

I wanted to join the army. I looked into this for a while, and eventually told my parents, giving them all the information they needed and I knew they would ask for. I thought this would not only teach me to be strong but it would be something that my parents would be proud of ... but without thinking about it both of them said "No, what if you don't come back to us alive?" I had no answer for this and realised that they still cared. Even though I had pretty much decided that this was my next step, I listened to my parents and I didn't pursue it.

> *"The weak can never forgive.*
> *Forgiveness is the attribute of the strong."*
> Mahatma Gandhi

Chapter 4
Starting from Scratch

A Healthy Lifestyle

I decided that I needed to take care of myself, and to rebuild myself again. Clear out the life that I knew, including the toxic people that came along with that. It was now time to think about me and what my next steps would be. I joined my local gym and started a few group classes like body conditioning and Pilates . . . I even took up boxing. I had so much anger and frustration to get rid of, which had built up in the last 5/6 years, that I felt like I was going to explode. I had so much suppressed anger and wanted to explode at every little thing . . . I didn't know how to deal with all the emotions. I started eating more salads and vegetables, and being a lot more active. At this point it was easy to focus on me as I had just finished my 3 year course at university. I went to the gym every day and also started to go to the sauna twice a week. I later found out that this helps to lose weight and get rid of the toxins . . . it was all about getting healthy. I found that I was shifting the weight and I was becoming more and more confident; my clothes started to feel looser. I started to notice that other people were noticing me . . . people would smile at me when I'm walking down the street and say morning, and I would smile and reply back. I remember one morning I was walking to the gym; it was a summer's day but with a slight breeze blowing. I had my jogging bottoms on with a vest top and a jacket and trainers on my way to the gym. There was a man at the cash point, casually dressed and looked ready for summer, who turned round and looked at me. I was walking in the same direction as he was, but he turned round and started to walk towards me. He was smiling at me and I smiled back; he then paused, looked at his hands and checked his pockets. He looked startled and rushed back to the cash point; he had forgotten to take the money that he withdrew from the machine. I smiled and giggled to myself; I was such a huge distraction that he even forgot to take his money!

I started to feel good about myself again. My confidence started to grow and I could feel that inner glow. I think it's called being happy! I also started to attend Muay Thai classes twice a week in the evenings. It was so much fun. I bought my gloves, shin pads, mouth guard and trainers. I thought to myself, I get to hit people, what a rush!!! I did boxing for a few months and heard about Thai boxing and decided to give it a go; it was a step up for me from boxing and now I got to kick people too! Boxing helped me with releasing the aggression and helped me to get fit at the same time.

As time went on I found myself taking on a lot more activities, including swimming lessons which was once a week. This was incredibly uncomfortable for me; even though I had lost a lot of weight, I still wasn't confident enough to wear a swimsuit. But if I didn't do this now then I would never do it, so I pushed myself out of my comfort zone and did a 12 week swimming course. To my surprise I noticed that I was getting better. I was able to swim a length without getting tired and stopping halfway. I felt amazing. So now I had a strong daily routine, gym in the morning, which meant a lot of cardio, treadmill, cross trainer, rowing boat, and the dreaded floor exercises, planks, squats, lunges . . . I hated doing these but they worked wonders. Afterwards I would either go to the sauna or to my Muay Thai classes depending on which day of the week it was and then after go straight home to eat . . . this was a perfect healthy lifestyle!

Never Judge a Book by its Cover

"Happiness depends on ourselves."
Aristotle

Gaining Employment

I then decided to sign on Job Seekers Allowance which is a form of unemployment benefit paid by the Government of the United Kingdom to people who are actively seeking work. Whilst I searched for a job and doing the mundane task of attending the Job Centre every 2 weeks, I also decided to register to a few Temp agencies where they specialise in recruiting people in admin roles and I applied for several jobs, but then there was this advert I saw on the internet and I wondered . . . should I or shouldn't I . . . surely I couldn't, it was a role to become a Special Constable!

"They will never take me on," I told myself. "Besides, isn't there a height requirement? I'm only 4ft 11inches. I will never be able to do this!" I filled out the application anyway, and sent it in!

I started to get bored at home and decided that I wanted to learn a new language ... but not French or Spanish that everyone usually learned. I wanted to be different and unique. I'm not much of a theory person but learn loads practically, so I decided to learn British Sign Language. Not many people learn this particular language; in fact I don't know anyone that can do this.

I also decided to do some volunteer work in order to gain experience, and in less than a month I was successful in gaining a role at my local Magistrates Court giving legal guidance. I enjoyed doing this on a part time basis, while I continued to look for a full time role. I was on top of the world. I had completed university, was working at a Magistrates Court, studying Sign Language and eating healthy and exercising . . . Life was good!

Whilst studying Sign Language I told my teacher that I didn't feel that I was learning quickly enough, and that I wanted to be confident in signing. She told me about a youth centre that had a club for young people who were deaf or hard of hearing, and that they were looking for people who could sign, and could work on Friday evenings. She went on to explain that if I surrounded myself with people who spoke any language, be it French, Spanish or Sign, I would pick up the language very quickly. She suggested that I express an interest, so I did.

And then it happened . . . I received a response from the Metropolitan Police, advising that they had accepted my application and inviting me to the first day assessment. If I passed the assessment I would then need to do the second day assessment and 18 weeks at the Academy. I was shocked and amazed . . . what should I do????

Within a week I got a call from one of the many agencies I had signed up to, and they told me that I had been accepted on a role, on a temporary but full time basis, as an administrator in a local college for 2 months. I accepted the position straight away although I knew that meant giving up volunteering at the Magistrates Court. I didn't think it could have gotten any better, but it did. I also passed my driving test, I am a full-fledged driver. I also found out that there was a permanent job advertised at the college, for the exact same position I was fulfilling on a temporary basis. I took this opportunity to apply for the permanent role. I took advise from my managers, who seemed really enthusiastic about me applying, and helped me with my application.

HR responded and told me that I had an interview. There were 3 posts available and there were 6 candidates: 4 males, myself and another girl, who was also a temp and worked with me. Two months had passed and both of our contracts got extended for another 2 months. This had to be a good sign right??? Just before Christmas break in November the director of the department, scary lady who seemed as tall as a giant and who never interacted with anyone on her team unless she was telling someone off, came over to me whilst I was working away at my PC. She whispered in my ear "HR wants to speak to you." I looked round, a little afraid, and asked why. "Do I need to take anything with me, like a notepad and pen?" She said 'no' and walked away.

I went to see HR, worried and un sure as to why they wanted to see me . . . I was sure I hadn't done anything wrong. HR presented me with a new contract for the permanent role . . . I had gotten the position! I was so excited, my hard work had paid off. 2008 was the best year; so much had happened and for the better. I felt like I was ready for the next stage.

Meeting New People

I was attending the gym and joined the Muay Thai, boxing, Pilates and body condition classes where I met people from different backgrounds and cultures . . . but I found that they were all in the same position as me. They were all uncomfortable with themselves and wanted to lose weight. Many of them were married with children and were struggling to find time for themselves, and few of them had a lot of other things going on that they were battling in their lives. There were two individuals in particular, who I became good friends with. Their names were Susan and Ty. Both of them had a child -- Susan a daughter and Ty a son, and both were young enough to be pushed around in a pram.

I got to know a lot of the staff at the gym because I went there every day. I knew the people at reception, membership lounge and the fitness instructors. I found that there was one particular fitness instructor who I spoke to a lot, about various things . . . life! Soon enough we started a relationship but due to him working at the gym we had to keep it on the down low.

Kourtney, my line manager at the Magistrates Court, was lovely. She was always there to help. I also worked with a guy named Emmet, who was Turkish and 6ft tall. He was a real funny and cocky person, although some would say he was arrogant. He was the same age as me and was looking for a full-time job also, and wanted to gain experience. He used to get into trouble with the manager all the time but he was harmless really!

I helped a lot of people prepare for their court hearing, and saw many people who were struggling with life and acting so inappropriately that they could potentially get in trouble with the law. I began to appreciated what I had! As a Special Constable I met many people including the Commissioner and Borough Commander . . . yes that's right I actually got into the Metropolitan police and I am now going out on the beat fighting criminals . . . I feel like I'm living a double life. My inspector was lovely. He supported his team so well, and was always ready to listen, no matter the time of day or night. My team was absolutely hilarious. I had never met a bunch so comical and yet so committed to their jobs. Honestly I didn't know how half of them found the time to go out on duty as a police officer, have a full time job and a family!!!

Working as a Youth Worker it was interesting to meet others who used sign language. I never realised that the deaf/ hard of hearing community was so huge. On my first day I met my manager. He was the type of manager that no one would ever want, the complete opposite to my inspector. He didn't have time to listen, and was rude and unappreciative. My colleagues were awesome and helped me improve my skills in sign language.

At the college this was my first full-time job after completing my studies and I was so excited. Even though it was just for the summer it was in the right direction for me. I had 2 line managers, Rita and Solomon, who worked together but were complete opposites. Rita was very unapproachable, cunning and walked around thinking she owned the college and could do nothing wrong. Whereas Solomon was very approachable and had time for his team, friendly and always smiling, and taking time out to talk to them to make sure that they were fine. Honestly he was my favorite! I worked with a huge team of 12 people but I bonded well with a Chinese girl called Mee Mee. We both started on the same day and it was also her first job after studying, we had found common ground.

Having a Social Life

As I started to get involved in different things I noticed that my social circle started to grow as well, and I hung out with different circles of people. I had a new boyfriend and new friends from the gym, colleagues at work that soon became my friends, and friends from Muay Thai and from the Met Police. I also kept in contact with those I worked with at the Magistrates Court, and I continued working at the Youth Centre Friday evenings. I had deaf/hard of hearing friends too that I would hang out with . . . this was an entirely different side of life that I walked into.

I attended parties with them that had very loud, horrible, head-banging music. I later found out that this was because they couldn't hear the music but danced to the vibrations on the floor . . . how amazing is that!

My boyfriend Damien and I used to meet up after work. Luckily enough the gym I attended was across the road from where I worked at the college, so it was very handy. I met with him before work, some days at lunch and after work, and again on the weekends. He even took me home to meet his family it was all going really well.

He also introduced me to his dermatologist, Gloria, who was a lovely person and very passionate about her job. She had designed the top floor of her house to be a beauty parlour and saw clients there. She became my dermatologist and started treating my skin as I suffered from acne. In time my skin improved and we became very good friends.

She had three daughters. The eldest was a year older than me and the other two were in secondary school. She invited me to her house for Christmas and for lunches, and we even went out shopping for clothes.

My two friends at the gym, Susan and Ty, always thought of me too, especially when inviting me to their kids' birthday parties. They were older than me by about 10 years, but I learnt a lot from them. Through their experiences they taught me a lot about life and marriage and kids; so much so that at that point I thought "Hell no, I'm not gonna get stuck in that kind of life . . . I have finally found my freedom, and I don't want to give that up!"

At the college Mee Mee and I continued to worked together. We hung out all the time at breaks and lunch, and we called each other after work. She even cooked a Chinese meal for me now and again for lunch, and in return I did the same with Indian food. Her favorite was the Okra curry however I only ever made that for her the once.

I also became very good friends with my supervisor, Teri. She was a very straightforward person. She didn't beat around the bush, but just told you as it was. She was also very knowledgeable and clever. She was single and full of energy. She was very supportive and pushed me to learn new skills. She was very good friends with Naomi, who was a mother of 3, her eldest being the same age as me. You would never think that she was as old as she was, due to all of the partying nights we used to have. We went out drinking, clubbing, and hung out at each other's houses watching movies and eating until we passed out.

My friends at Muay Thai were always talking about eating healthy; a lot of them were trying to go pro and had to watch what they ate and drank, but we did have a few nights out at a restaurant in Goodmayes where it was designed as though you were eating in a boxing ring. There were framed photos of famous people who had also eaten at the restaurant. It was nothing like I had ever seen. Once, the manager closed the restaurant and we had our very own private party. I even got behind the bar and pretended to be Peggy Mitchell from Eastenders. It was a fun night.

All of us at the Met police had frequent meetings in the evening but they often turned out to be a little picnic party around a huge table. My neighbour Anita, who I had known since I was a year old, also worked for the Met and we became even better friends. Through her I met two other girls, Parveen and Aysha, and the four of us became very good friends. We used to go out and try new restaurants, and we even decided to go on holiday together to the Czech Republic. I was so nervous, because this was my first holiday with friends and no family and I even started packing 2 months in advance just to make sure I had everything I needed. We booked 2 rooms; Anita and Parveen shared a room and I shared with Aysha. Parveen was the most sensible one and also very calm; she never got angry and always found a solution. Aysha was all about the way she looked; her hair and makeup had to be perfect and it took her hours to get ready in the mornings. It was only a four day trip but it felt like we did and saw everything. Parveen and I even went shooting . . . yeah they actually trusted us with guns!

Finding me again!

With all the attempts to better myself, starting from scratch gaining experience, meeting new people and building friendships and relationships, I definitely found that I was becoming someone else, someone new. It was almost like I was getting to know me again. I started to understand that my experiences will always remain with me, but they have only made me a stronger person, more willing to try new things and to never settle for what I know. I was having loads of fun sharing time with the various circles of friends I now had . . .each circle was very different from one another but each and every one made up a part of me.

From my past I learnt that I was a very patient person, but I came to realise that there were certain things that I just wouldn't stand for anymore. I had seen the signs and would keep well away from them. I was well on my way to finding out what kind of person I was, and what I would and would not tolerate, but I also knew that there was so much more for me to learn. I was totally ready for it!

I started to learn my worth, and realized that I was not an awful person, as I had continuously been told in the past. The people I had around me liked hanging out with me, and we always made each other smile. I learnt to be strong. In fact I was actually stronger than I had thought. I learnt that I will make mistakes . . . but that I would always get through them and come out on top. I learnt that life isn't all about drinking and smoking and hanging out on the streets . . .

There was so much I want to do and experience and I will not let anything or anyone stop me, I was determined to push for what I want. I was also feeling pretty again, when I looked in the mirror I wasn't seeing this ugly, fat person anymore. I was feeling a lot more confident with all aspects of my life, I was seeing a huge improvement within myself. In a single year 2008, I had completed my degree at university, gained a full time and permanent job at the college, passed my driving licence, became fluent in another language, lost weight, and my skin improved as well, I ate a lot healthier, got a second job with the Met Police and gained new friendships. I had proved to myself that I was capable of anything but at the same time I think back and realised that I wasted do much time in those five years, I felt like now I had to play catch up and make up for all those years that I wasted . . . just imagine what I could have accomplished, I found that I started questioning myself but shook the negative thoughts away and I had to tell myself that this is now time for me to move forward, that this was just an obstacle in which I learnt a hard lesson. I also learnt something else about myself, that in times of distress, I had to keep myself occupied and found that I became obsessed with cleaning but I found this very therapeutic and was able to be in my own thoughts.

> "We cannot solve our problems with the same thinking we used when we created them."
> Albert Einstein

Chapter 5
Learning Curves

The Working Life

My job at the college was my first full-time permanent job since university. I was so excited and couldn't wait to make money . . . I felt all grown up. My first mission was to pay off my student loan as soon as possible, and put a lump sum aside every month. I successfully paid my debt in 2 years. In 2011 I was debt free, and I had learnt a lot of lessons from working at the college.

Many of the managers didn't really have a clue what they were doing or even how to speak to staff appropriately. It was the people at the bottom that ran around making sure that everything ran as it was supposed to, with no appreciation from management . The only appreciation you got was a box of chocolates for the team and that was if you were lucky.

It was clear to me that there was no room for me to be promoted. There was a day when a student came in to enrol on the course. He had been told by another department, a department that had no idea how benefits worked, that he could enrol in a course for free, and when he came to me and showed me his benefit letters he actually had to pay. Of course the student was not happy, so I took him with me to speak to the person who told him he could have the course for free. This other member of staff was seeing another student, so we waited. He waved us to come forward and I explained to him the situation and that's when it went all out of hand. He started shouting at the student; he stood up from his seat and squared up to him. The student spoke poor English and was frightened, and couldn't understand why he was being shouted at. I couldn't believe what I was seeing. I pulled the student away and took him out of the room . . . I repeatedly apologised to him and said that the other staff member should never have spoken to him like that. Not surprisingly, he no longer wanted to attend a course with us, and he left. I told my managers about what had happened and they asked me to write up a report. I sent it to them via email. A few days later the director of my department approached me and told me that he had heard about what had happened, and he agreed that this was no way to speak to a student. He advised me that I could take it to HR, but he couldn't guarantee what the end result would be. I asked if he could guarantee that I would still have my job if I went to HR about this, and his reply was 'no'! I decided that it was not worth losing my job over but at the same time I knew that it wasn't right.

This bothered me for a while, which is why I decided to become a Union Representative. I would stand up for what was right. I helped many people with their cases but at the same time I felt like I was making enemies with management. They didn't like that fact that there now was someone helping people, a voice speaking up. I attended meetings with the Executives and Principalship, especially during redundancies, and I helped many staff members to save their jobs, even if it meant re-applying for their own roles or applying for other roles in the college. It made me feel so good that I was able to help people; it was a sense of satisfaction, an overwhelming feeling. I carried on helping people in different situations for 3 years after.

The Family Life & My Social Circle of Friends

We went on a few family holidays. First we decided to go away to Centre Parks. We decided that it would be fun for us all to get involved in a few activities and try things we have never done before. My brother and I had a go at the high ropes, which was a huge deal for him as he was afraid of heights. Because it was a huge park with loads of activities at different ends, and no cars were allowed, the only form of transportation was by bike. Neither my mum nor I could ride a bike so my dad decided to rent out tricycles for the both of us. It was hilarious. I seemed to be getting on with my parents a lot better than previously.

There was a year where we flew to Turkey, which was a completely different holiday to our previous one. Firstly this was abroad and in the sun. It was a more relaxing holiday where we chilled out by the pool and went for strolls, although we did get involved in some activities such as quad biking and Jeep Safari. We celebrated everyone's birthday and went to different restaurants that we wanted to try out. We all took the day off from work and celebrated my brother's graduation, we went to eat and have a few drinks and the day seemed to go by quickly. In the past mum and I had mother and daughter days out to either a spa, afternoon tea or on occasion both on one trip. We had attended so many spas around London that I can say that we would have made awesome spa critiques. One of the days we even had a spa day on a yacht which was pretty spectacular. Whilst my mum and I went and got ourselves pampered on these days out, my dad and younger brother used to spend these days either going bowling or playing snooker and to finish the day off wit a few drinks a typical boys day out. During the weekday we all gather around the TV in the living room and watched all the usual British soaps Eastenders, Coronation Street and Emmerdale. During the weekend we all did the chores in the house and we have certain rooms in the house that we are in charge of. I cleaned the kitchen and the bathroom, my dad cleans the living room and the staircase, my brother cleans the room upstairs whilst my mum goes and does the weekly shopping.

Previously we had discussed that it would be nice to go and do some sightseeing and do some touristy stuff during the summer season. I suggested that we go to London Zoo and my dad started laughing, I asked why is that funny, is it because you think I'm too old to enjoy the zoo, he said no, that was the place I took your mum on our first date and we all started laughing and my brother and I thought this would be a perfect family day out and it would give my parents the opportunity to go down memory lane. I also spent some time with my nan and went to visit her as often as I could, we had to bring her bed down to the living room from upstairs as she had problems with her knees and struggled to climb the stairs. My nan's bed was so cosy that every time I went to visit her I jumped on her bed and got under the covers. I had told her even if you don't see me as often as you like that she is always in my thoughts which is why no matter where I am in the world she always receives a gift from me on my return. In fact my nan even had the cheek to tell me that I don't need to buy her anything as when she passes, I will end up getting them back anyway . . . how morbid! That didn't stopped me she still got bombarded with loads of gifts.

I started to meet new people and socialised with a lot of the friends I made at work, Teri and Naomi loved to have barbeques and invite people round; they never really needed an excuse to have a barbecue. We also went to a few clubs in London, which was always entertaining. I started to travel abroad with my friends Anita and Parveen; we have been to so many amazing places on the other side of the world. I also attended an annual event with the Met Police every year for five years, where we raised money for Cancer In Kids, otherwise known as Jack's Pack (Joining Against Cancer In Kids – Police Against Cancer In Kids). I travelled with Kirsty who also worked for the Suffolk Police. We were in uniform and completed a plane pull at JFK Airport in New York and ran a half marathon in half uniform from the waist up. It was challenging but completely fun. I visited most of the States in the USA with Kirsty. We both loved America, and found that every state was different to one another, it almost felt like we had stepped into a completely different country.

Even though I had different circles of friends who enjoyed different things, all those things were also what I enjoyed, and each of them was an element of who I was and together it made me who I am. This included my family.

Who am I and What do I want?

I am someone who likes to be organised and plan everything in my life, but I have come to realise that plans don't always work out the way they should, and life likes to surprise you in many ways. It sometimes will be bad but at other times will be great. Either way there seems to be some sort of lesson that you need to learn. I do believe that everything happens for a reason. I have a list of things I want to experience and I was so eager to reach my full potential. All I need is for someone to give me the opportunity to show them what I can do. I am compassionate, helpful and an optimist. I am learning that even though there may be many things around me that seem to be going wrong, there is still hope. I am a fighter and don't want to give up on the things I dream about. I believe that my time will come, but I just need to continue to work hard and to be patient. I want to have control of my life; it only makes sense. No one else should have control of my life. I am a pretty confident person although there are days that I doubt myself. I am willing to learn from others to gain the knowledge I need to better myself. I will do what it takes to just to be one step closer to what I want. I will keep on trying and I won't stop until I have achieved everything I want.

Kalpna Suthar

"A pessimist sees the difficulty in every opportunity; an optimist sees the opportunity in every difficulty."
Winston Churchill

I want a job that I am passionate about, so that it no longer feels like a job. I want to wake up every morning looking forward to the day and not dreading it. I want to work with people that appreciate me, and who are positive and not just looking out for themselves but also for their team. I want to feel like I am working as part of a true team. I want to be financially stable and to be able to buy a house for myself. I want to be able to tell my mum that she no longer has to work and that I can take care of her, especially as I see her struggling every day with her arthritis. I want to be able to afford to take my family on holiday to places they never thought they would ever see but have always spoken about. I want to set an example for my brother and to help him to pay off his student loan for his degree and masters, so he doesn't have to worry about paying it off like I did. I want to travel all over the world and experience things that I otherwise wouldn't have been able to do and to meet like-minded people. I want to grow as a person and be the best I can be, because I know I have the potential to help people all around the world and to be able to relate. I want to own a business and employ those that have great potential; I want them to look forward to coming to work for me. I won't end up being anything like those managers that I had in the past, ignorant and condescending. In fact, I have learnt a lot from those people, about the kind of person or manager I don't want to become. I don't want to be just a manager; I want to be a leader, and a role model. I want to inspire everyone I come in contact with and when they leave I want to leave them with a great feeling.

Ultimately I want to make a difference in the world.

Never Judge a Book by its Cover

"Without reflection, we go blindly on our way, creating more unintended consequences, and failing to achieve anything useful."
Margaret J. Wheatley

Chapter 6
Wanting More

Employment Progression

I had tried so hard to apply for a promotion within the college but had no luck. I tried to progress with the Met Police as they were having a huge recruitment drive, but as I put my application through it was publicised that the recruitment had been put on hold for 2 years . . . it was just my luck. Even when I thought I proved myself by taking on more responsibilities and tasks as a supervisor, and had been totally committed for six months, when it came to offering me a permanent role, doing exactly the same things as I was currently doing, they told me that I came across as "ghetto" in my interview . . . can you believe that?

I was really stunned. I never thought this would be the kind of feedback I would get. I was annoyed too, as it felt like they had no reasonable reason not to give me the job, and this was the only thing they could come up with. I applied for several more positions outside of my department but I wasn't even given an interview for them, even though I got help from HR to fill out my application. I also started to look online for different roles and registered with several employment agencies. I kept searching but found that there wasn't much out there.

As I wanted a management role but didn't have the experience of the qualification, I enrolled on to a management course, and worked through my assignments during my lunch break, after work and on the weekends. It took me about 4 months, and then I completed the course with flying colours and received my certificate. I then used this to apply for further management roles thinking that at my interviews they would be so impressed and hire me but unfortunately these qualifications still didn't get me anywhere.

As I didn't have the qualifications in Event Management I also decided to get qualified in this as well, and received my certificate, the way I understood it was even though I wasn't currently getting the roles I wanted, the more qualifications I had couldn't hurt. Soon I was flying to New York with the Met Police, raising money for Cancer In Kids. Kirsty and I thought about different ways to raise the funds. We decided to hold a fete for children, and the theme would be the Police force, which combined the different forces in the UK including Metropolitan, Suffolk and Essex police. We managed to plan and organise this event and even got a part in the local Suffolk newspaper. We worked on this fete in every spare time we could find, keeping in mind that we both had full-time jobs. We recruited volunteers, hired a venue, which happened to be an old tudor castle, we arranged for advertising, marketing and catering, and we rented a bouncy castle, a rodeo and even managed to get a load of things for our raffle. We had someone bake us a special Jack's Pack cake, for the event. We hired a live band and were able to get a few police vehicles down for the children. It was a lovely venue and had a small farm for the children as well. We had police directing cars to the car park and patrolling the whole event. We had raised a lot more than expected and the manager of the venue was so pleased, as she received such huge publicity that she told us that we didn't need to pay her for the venue. Many parents told us that they felt safe for their children to run around without having to worry . . . well I'm not surprised they felt safe . . . everywhere you looked there were police officers.

After the event Kirsty and I were so proud of ourselves; even though it was a lot of work it was all worth it in the end. This was my first successful event.

Helping People

I became very grateful for what I had in my world; for the house I lived in, for my health, family and friends, for being able to work and go away and travel, for the food I ate and the clean water I could drink.

I noticed a man who hung around down the high street; I saw him every day during my lunch break . He was homeless and even though there were quite a few homeless people around in that area he was the one that stood out. He was the only one who never begged or asked passersby for money or anything else. He always had a shopping trolley with him, full of black bags which were packed full of his belongings. The bags were piled up quite high and it almost looked as though the trolley would tip over. He had layers of clothes on and they were all very dirty. He had a beard which didn't look very healthy either, and I had decided that the next time I saw him I would buy him some food. I thought about buying the food and just giving it to him, but he was Pakistani, and I wondered if there were only certain foods he would eat. So I went out during my lunch break and I saw him coming out of the public toilets. I decided to approach him, I asked him how his day had been and he said "It's hard; it's hard on the streets." His name was Akbar. I told him that I would like to buy him some food from across the road which was a fast food store but to my astonishment he said he didn't eat fast food. He then went on to say that he only ate halal food, and that fast food really wasn't very healthy to eat. My eyebrows raised. I couldn't believe that this man, who lived out on the streets, went through bins to look for food and anything else he could get his hands on, was telling me that fast food was too unhealthy for him! I then asked him if I could get him fish and chips, but he still refused. When I asked him what he would like, he turned and looked at me and said "I would be happy for you to gave me a job, such as sweeping your floors, carrying any rubbish from your house to your bin, so that I can receive money to buy some food. It was clear . . . he was a man of integrity. He didn't want anything for free, and was willing to work regardless of what the job was. This told me a lot about him, and I was intrigued. I wanted to know more about him. I asked him how he ended up here and his story was so heartfelt. He told me that he had been a director in an accounting firm in central London, and had been a loyal employee for years. The company had gone into liquidation, and he had searched for another job for months, but was unsuccessful. He eventually lost his flat as he wasn't able to keep up with his rent payments. I asked him about his family . . . he said to me, "I learnt a lot about family, and it's sad to say but they were the first to turn their backs on me when they saw the hardship I was in. When I was doing well . . . they didn't leave my side. although I have a huge family that live all over the world not one gave me a helping hand when I needed it the most."

My heart went out to Akbar. I asked him how long he had been out on the streets and he replied "4 years." He went on to say that the streets were horrible, and that he had seen his best friend burn to death. He said that some drunks thought it would be funny to pour petrol over him and set him on fire one night after they had finished from the local pub. My mouth dropped!

He was also a very intelligent man and told me that he spoke 11 different languages. He named all eleven and somehow he knew that my second language was Gujarati and asked me how I was in Gujarati. I replied back in Gujarati. I had been speaking to him for over 30 minutes. I told him that I was happy to buy him some food, but again he refused. I went on to tell him that I needed to get back to work as I was on my lunch break. He understood and thanked me for talking to him, and asked me to speak to him whenever I saw him. I said goodbye and went back to work. I was tearful at this stage. He had everything and then came across some bad luck and lost everything, and he had no one to help him. He was an intelligent man, and had very unique skills that most people didn't have. He didn't deserve to be on the streets. In fact no one does.

I started reflecting on how lucky I was. I wanted to do something.

> *"Try to be a rainbow in someone's cloud."*
> Maya Angelou

More Time and Money

I wished I had more time to do what I wanted. I would have loved to put the time in planning and organising events, all sorts of events. I was even happy to do this on a voluntary basis; it really didn't matter to me as long as I was working on an event. I thought about starting my own Events and Wedding Planning business, and with that create a programme for the homeless. I would give them a job and a place to live, and allow them to earn money for themselves, help them get back into the community, and give them hope.

I wanted to buy a huge house, actually no . . . a mansion with black metal gates and drive through and in the centre as you reach up to the door there is a huge water fountain. A white Range rover with cream interiors. I wanted to be able to tell my mum that she didn't have to work anymore, and she could enjoy staying at home and relaxing. I wanted to be able to pay for my brother's tuition fees and to put some money away for him. I also wanted to be able to pay for my parents' mortgage, and I wanted to get on to the property ladder and own several properties. I wanted to be able to take my family away on holiday, to places they never thought they would ever to go due to the high prices.

Kirsty told me that the tudor castle that we had out fete. The manager wanted to sell it for nine million pounds. A light bulb went off in my head. If I could purchase that venue I could hold several different events, including weddings. There was even a little cottage that could become the honeymoon suite . . . it would be perfect, and I could do so much with it. But there was a huge factor that was missing . . . the money. There was no way I could raise it in the short amount of time required. But I guess I can still dream about that day.

I wanted to spend time doing the things that make me happy, and not working Monday to Friday waiting for the weekend to arrive. I wanted to only do the things that make me happy. I no longer want to waste my time going through the motions and falling in a rut.

I wanted to be able to travel and not have to worry about having enough money . . . I wanted to be able make a decision in one split second about going away and not having to think about whether or not I would be able to get the time off and wait until my leave has been authorised or worse . . . if it is denied then I would not be able to travel, to have that doctors appointment, or dentist appointment and then request time off again and it being added to your records and generally being micromanaged by people who are completely incompetent with their own jobs let alone manage a team. I want to be able to decided what time I want to go to lunch and whether or not it's a good time for me to visit the GP, not because the company haven't got enough staff due to their own fault and making all the essential people redundant and passing the caseload on everyone who's left.

Running Away from Life

In the Summer of 2014 I went to visit my friend Kirsty and stayed with her for a few days, she lived in Suffolk, UK. Both of us felt like we had hit rock bottom . . . we had tried so hard to progress in terms of our careers. She wanted to become a full-time police officer in Suffolk and she had tried several times. Every time her application had been declined. I had tried different avenues of progression at work but I kept hitting my head against the brick wall. I knew I could do any job I was given, and do a great job. All I needed was someone to give me a chance.

We decided to go to the local pub which was 2 minutes away from Kirsty's place. It was a cute place; it looked like a cottage. The staff seemed to know a lot of the people there, so they must have been loyal customers. It was a friendly place, where everyone smiled at you; not like London at all.

As we sat there reminiscing about the past and checking the order menu, we started talking about our future. We couldn't believe the number of knockbacks we had received. We then started talking about what we really wanted from life. If we could do anything, what would it be?

After talking for a few hours, not even noticing the time go by we had a light bulb moment . . . we realized we had nothing to stay in the UK for; we were not married or even in a relationship, and we had no kids. We were completely free to do whatever we wanted . . . the world was our oyster.

We then thought about working on P&O cruises. I could work on the events team and Kirsty could work as Security. We were so excited! We could start all over again and meet new people whilst travelling around the world. This would be a great opportunity and a way to get away from all of our troubles.

Kirsty invited me to come down quite often, and in that same year during the summer where her parents flew to Spain and she invited me to stay with her a few days and this time she invited Penny too. Penny also worked in the Metropolitan Police force and had done for several years but she was based in an entirely different borough to me. All three of us decided to go a for a walk near the river and we had found a free bench and decided to take a seat and look over at the river. We started discussing life and what it would be like if we had everything we ever wanted. Kirsty and I were working on our career whereas Penny was looking at ways to move to America even if it meant doing it immorally. She was in a dark place more so than Kirsty and I. We were all in the same boat I guess and we were all looking at ways of running from where we currently were.

> *"You will never do anything in this world without courage. It is the greatest quality of the mind next to honor."*
> Aristotle

Chapter 7
Brand New Me – 'Miss Fabulous!'

Personal Coach

Five years passed. It was 2014, and I hated myself . . . the way I looked, the way I felt. My clothes didn't look right, my jeans were tight . . . I didn't even wear dresses anymore because I looked like a cheeseball. How did I end up back here again? I was doing so well with the gym and eating healthy.

I had gone on holiday to Turkey with my family the previous summer, and I hated every photo I was in as I looked so fat!!!!

I hated my job where I worked at the college. I had worked there for many years and tried so hard but I found that management didn't care how great you worked . . . if your face didn't fit you weren't going to get anywhere in the company. They employed family and friends, and looked after them, even if they did their job badly.

My supervisor, Teri, announced that she was leaving because she found a better job. She had taught me so much over the years that I decided that I would prove that I was worthy of being a supervisor. For about 4 months I worked on the tasks that as a supervisor, and decided I would apply for the role once it was sent out.

An internal advert was sent out for the position. I sent in my application form and was told I was going to have an interview.

There were 5 other people who had also applied. I thought I was bound to get it. . . I had been doing the role for 6 months, and none of the managers had complained. They must like my work, right? Wrong!!!!Two weeks went passed, and I found out that I did not get the position. In fact none of the 5 of us got it!!! I was upset and felt that all my hard work was pointless. I asked for feedback and to my shock there wasn't a thing that they could tell me,

I later found out that they had given the position to someone who didn't apply for the job, someone who didn't even want it, just because they were already on that pay scale and then had the cheek to ask me to train this person up. "Sorry, but if I'm not good enough for the position then I certainly am not good enough to train them," I said to myself.

When I returned from Turkey I decided that something had to be done to change that way I looked and felt. I was unhappy with every aspect of my life. One evening as I was browsing through my facebook, I came across a post about losing weight in a 12 week programme. As I read on it stated that in 12 weeks you could learn about nutrition.

The 12 week programme had begun . . .

Sunday 3rd August 2014
Today was the first day of my 4 day detox and it was a struggle! I had to stop myself from picking up a biscuit, fruit or my all time favorite, hula hoops. It was the end of the day and although I didn't enjoy my first meal of the day . . . green salad ... I stuck to the plan and I did it . . . Bring on tomorrow!!!

Monday 4th August 2014
Today was day 2 of my detox and it felt harder then yesterday but only because I was I work. One of the hardest part of the day

was towards lunch when everyone in the office started talking about what they are having for lunch . . . All I could think about was biting into a sandwich! And then it happened . . . I went to lunch with a colleague and she decided to have Subway for lunch, it smelt heavenly but I can quite happily say that I resisted. There were a couple obstacles today but day 2 is now successfully complete!

Tuesday 5th August 2014
So today was day 3 of my detox and whilst it gets easier for some, for me it feels the complete opposite. I've been thinking about food all day . . . The kebabs, burgers, chips, pepperoni pizzas. I've even had someone scream at me today . . . My belly . . . It was so angry she was screaming for food and surprisingly today has been the first day I've had a headache. But the one major difference this detox has already had, is that I've been having the best sleep. It has been a struggle, but I DID IT!!! And the one thing I'm now looking forward to is tomorrow the final day of my detox . . . Its almost over . . . Bring it!!!

Wednesday 6th August 2014
Yay . . . Today was the final day of my detox. It was hard, there was a lot of temptation but I did it. I'm so relieved that its over, it definitely got harder as the days went on. But I'm so glad that I got through it. Can't wait for tomorrow . . . So excited, I can finally eat a full meal!!!

Thursday 7th August 2014
It was my first day of training with my coach and all I can say is OMG!!! There was a lot of sweat and pain & I even threw up . . . Just when I thought there was no hope & I couldn't go on any longer . . . My coach tapped into something amazing! She told me to close my eyes and to think about a point in my life where I felt good about myself, a time where I achieved something . . . To my shock whilst I was on my 2nd set, still having my eyes

closed, I was doing better then I did on my 1st set. You maybe wondering why this is and how that is possible . . . Well whilst I had my eyes closed. . . I was thinking about a day that I was in school and it was sports day. I put my name down to do the obstacle race and then was disheartened when I realised that I was up against 3 boys, but to everyone's shock I had the last laugh, I had WON!

Thursday 14th August 2014
Ok so I'm a week and a half into my 12 week programme and have lost 3lbs already . . . Yay! The only major change I have made so far is the foods I've been eating, more veg, fruit and a whole load of protein. Lets see if I can shake off another 2lbs by the end of the month . . . Watch this space!!!

Sunday 17th August 2014
This morning whilst eating my super healthy breakfast my brother asked me if I had lost any more weight . . . I told him that I think that the scales in the bathroom are broken . . . he naturally laughed and said "I take that as a no then". I explained that I stepped on the scales and it showed me that I was over 9 stones and then I stepped off and then stepped back on and then showed that I was 8.5 stones, therefore it isn't giving me an accurate reading. So at this point I felt low and don't think that I have lost anything in the last 2 weeks even though I have been eating a lot more healthier and exercising!!! I headed off to see me physiotherapist and saw that she had scales in her consultation room and asked if they are working and if I could use them . . . to my shock I had lost over half a stone in just 2 weeks . . . I couldn't believe it, I even stepped off and stepped back on just to make sure and it gave me the same reading. Loosing over half a stone, 8.8lbs to be exact, (for those that don't know there's 14lbs in 1 stone) in just 2 weeks feels amazing . . . I am FABULOUS, Thanks to my coach. Let's see if I can reach to a full stone in the next 2 weeks . . . watch this space!!!

The one thing I always looked forward to was when I finished work . . . not because I was finally out of that hell hole of a place I call work but because I was going training almost everyday after work with my coach . . . she was another source of boost and every time I met her I would learnt something else that was useful and through her I learnt a lot about myself . . . she was a breathe of fresh air, the light at the end of the tunnel. There were many times during my session where I had a heart to heart with my coach and I had broken down in tears . . . what you need to understand is that she was not only a Fitness training she also helped people to love themselves again, she worked with people to improve their inner wellbeing as well as the external parts of the body . . . and that is why she is called my coach . . . she coached me on my fitness, nutrition, she taught me the foods my body needs and the foods I should avoid . . . she even went as far as tell me to go to my doctor and get myself checked out and then worked with me on my own specific needs. I found that I had a lot of internal problems and that's where she helped me . . . she explained that I need to work on myself from the inside before the outside or I will not see the changes on the outside . . . so for 12 weeks I was on this journey of working on myself.

Positive Thinking

My coach implemented having a positive mindset to the training and asked me to read a book called The Secret. To be honest it all sounded a bit too far-fetched, this whole positive thinking thing, but she had helped me so much already, and I was desperate to get out of this rut and feeling so down that I was willing to try anything.

I looked into purchasing the book but found that there was a DVD. I thought this would be a much better option for me as I didn't have the motivation to read a book, or even the time for it.

I received the DVD through the post, and one night I put my pyjamas on and sat on my bed, ready to watch this in my bedroom. When it first started I was thinking "This is going to be the longest and most painful movie I have ever watched." But as I kept watching, things started to make sense. By the end of the DVD I felt like I could achieve anything that I wanted. I hadn't felt like this for a long time.

Slowly I started to implement certain things in my daily life that had been mentioned in the movie, but as I was in such a delicate stage in my life I didn't feel like I had the strength to keep it up. I decided that it would help me to keep focus if I watched The Secret, the last thing that I watched before I went to bed and the first thing I watched when I got up.

I did this for about a month . . . I always felt so good after watching this DVD. It helped to remind me to think about all the positive things in my life. So when I went into work and I started thinking about good things . . . and started thinking about what I wanted. What did I want to do? Where did I see myself in five years?

I discovered that the reason I was stuck in this rut was because I didn't know what I wanted to do, therefore I had no sense of direction or push. I started doing a lot of thinking about what made me happy . . . the experiences in the past that I had enjoyed and things that I hadn't enjoyed so much.

There was an aspect of my working life that I knew I had to change . . . being a Special Constable! This had become a burden, and I decided that if anything made me feel like this it was time to get out.

I handed in my resignation in October 2014. Also at that time, I had to go into hospital for an operation. Everything went well and I was placed in recovery. The nurses came into the room every 20 minutes to check on me and make sure everything was back to normal before they released me. They were not happy with my recovery as my heart rate was slower than it should have been. I told them that I felt fine but they asked me to stay longer, until my heart rate picked up. Over an hour went by, and they still couldn't understand why my heart rate was slower than the average person. Three different nurses came in to check my heart rate, and one of them asked me if I exercised. When I replied 'yes' she asked how many times a week. I said 5-7 times a week. And then she said "That is why your heart rate is so slow; you have a heart rate of a professional athlete." At this point I knew that I had sorted out any issues that had been holding me back with my body . . . it was so good to know that I worked so hard to fix me and it was all worthwhile . . . I was so grateful to my coach who had helped me get to this point. My body was now in its best shape possible . . . finally!!!

My Vision Board

My coached asked me if I had put up a vision board, but I hadn't don't it yet. She told me to go and buy a cork board and to think about the things I wanted in my life. She told me that my board could be as extravagant as I wanted it to be. I thought about what I wanted, but none of it was really making much sense, the things I wanted was so random that I had no idea how I could possibly have it all!

The next day at my training session I told her how I was feeling about the vision board and she told me that it didn't have to make sense. All I had to know was that I wanted it. Once I started focusing on the things that I wanted, they would manifest and the universe would present them to me, again this all sounded so far fetched.

So on the weekend I started searching online for pictures of the things that I wanted. For years I had no idea what I wanted to do as a career and then during my time at the college it came to me like a flood, I felt like I found my niche . . . I wanted to work in events, so I typed up 'events management' and put that on my board. I typed up 'I Am Fabulous' and put that there as well. As I searched for images to do with wealth I came across a picture of a one million pound note . . . I never knew that there was such a thing. I printed all the images I saw on the internet, and stuck them on my vision board. I put it in my bedroom in the perfect place, where it was the first thing I saw when I got up and the last thing when I went to bed.

That night I had a dream. It was very intense, and felt very real. I woke up the next day feeling pumped and excited. I dreamt that I had left working for the college and I was managing my very own events company . . . I was so well-known in the industry that I even managed to get David Beckham to open up my event . . . that was huge! The Principle at the college I worked at also heard about my event and attended. She was so impressed that she asked around to find out who had organised the event. Eventually she realised that it was me, and all of a sudden she wanted to know all about me. She started talking to me like I was her best friend. She asked me to come back and work at the college again, but this time in Events. I very quickly told her that I was not interested and walked away.

"If you can dream it, you can do it."
Walt Disney

Being Grateful

One evening when I went for my training session after work my coach told me that she had a gift for me . . . I automatically thought "Oh no, she will probably get me to do an extra 20 push-ups or do the dreaded suicide drills" . . . because that's the kind of person she was. She would push all of her clients to prove that they could do it, that they were strong enough. She would get you to open your eyes to see that you were not weak. To my shock that wasn't my gift. She went into her bag and pulled out a little blue book. When she opened it up it was completely blank. The sheets of paper were lined and she told me that she had got this book for me to write down all the things that I was grateful for, and that I should start doing this on a daily basis. I looked at her unsure and she told me that I was to write every little thing that I was grateful for, such as my eyesight, heath, and being able to do the 12 week training programme. I mentioned that this was what they talked about in The Secret. "Yes," she replied. "Now it's time for you to think about all the good you have around you."

So every day for a couple weeks I wrote about all the things I was grateful for. I started listing everything, the people I had met, how they had helped me, my family, being able to travel, my health, the places I'd visited. One morning I got a text from my coach, asking me to ask 3 people about what they thought were 3 of my strengths and 3 of my weaknesses. At first I thought this was strange; how was I expected just to ask 3 people these random questions? But I went to work that morning and I just put it out there, and asked everyone in the office what they thought my weaknesses and strengths were. I was shocked by their responses. Every person in the office said that my biggest strength was being confident . . . my jaw dropped. I never saw myself as being a confident person; I'd always thought that I was indecisive and nervous all the time. Then they said that I was determined and motivated. When it came to my weaknesses they couldn't think of 3, but they all said that there was one particular weakness; that I was not tactful and I didn't think about what I said and just told people straight. I thought about this and I didn't actually see this as a weakness -- I'm just a straightforward type of person -- but then I thought about it again. Clearly I must have said something in the past that they didn't like, and have held this inside for some time, but they never thought to mention it to me. I was so shocked that people actually saw me as being confident; I was not sure that this was true, and I texted about 4 people and asked them the same question. It was strange that they couldn't think of a weakness but again all said that my strengths were being confident, determined and motivated.

After work that evening I told my coach about this and she smiled. This gave me a huge boost to do even better. Realising that this was how people saw me showed me that I saw myself in a completely different light. When I got home I got my little blue book out and started writing that I was grateful for the way people saw me, as I had no idea that this was how I came across to others. No matter how much I tried and how many knock backs that I got, I still carried on and focused on my dreams and my wants. I didn't stop writing down everything I was grateful for, even though I had bad days at work there were still plenty of things around me that I was grateful for. At the end of the day, things happen for a reason. There were days when I was down, but changing my mindset to the positive always helped me to get out of that funk. One night I had a dream. I had won the lottery . . . I won ninety-one million pounds . . . I was so shocked and overwhelmed but frustrated that I couldn't see the numbers I picked out in my dream. I woke up telling my mum that if only I could see the numbers, I could possibly be a lottery winner and a millionaire. But then I decided that million pound note that I had put on my vision board previously to change it and I added a 9 in front of the 1, so it now read ninety one million pounds... "Let's see how this pans out!" I said to myself.

Loving Myself Again

I felt different, happier, things didn't seem so bad anymore. Of course I wasn't doing exactly what I wanted yet, but I definitely saw a change with my inner wellbeing. I saw things in a positive light, and I was so grateful for my job at the college -- it was how I could pay for all the things I loved: going travelling, meeting friends, trying out new restaurants, going shopping and buying the health foods that I can cook and eat. Without my job I wouldn't have been able to do these things. As I realised that being grateful and focusing on the positives works, I also started realising that there was a true meaning behind affirmations . . . they are not just sayings as I thought they were.. I started to think outside the box, and when I went on facebook and saw certain affirmations it made me think! I starting seeing more affirmations than ever before.

2015 let me re-introduce myself!

As the new year came around I decided that there was now a new me, and I related very well to Alicia Keys' song "Brand New Me." I listened to it again and again. I had completed my 12 week programme with my coach and I had lost 2 stones altogether that's 28bls, just under 13kgs. I felt so much better about myself, more confident and I now believed in myself . . . I was ready to change my life. I decided to get involved in things that made me enjoy life . . . so I enrolled in a 12 week dance class, where professional dancers taught people different dance routines, at different levels.

When I got there on the first day there were so many people there that I got nervous and felt uncomfortable. Everyone there looked like they had been dancing for years. But I decided that I wouldn't let fear hold me back, so I stayed. As the weeks went on my confidence grew. I made friends with one of the girls there, who was previously a ballet dancer but who wanted to experience other dance styles. As the weeks went on I had made friends with a lot of the others dancers in my class and after one session a bunch of us decided that we should go round the corner to grab something to eat, and I had an amazing time. It was a revelation and I definitely left in high spirits. It's funny how last-minute decisions can turn into some sort of a purpose . . . especially as most of us didn't really know each other that well just through the dance classes but yet we all had several other things in common.

From then on I always looked forward to going to my dance classes; even though I was always a couple steps behind everyone else . . . we all just laughed! There were a few nerve-racking moments when the dance instructor chose me and a couple others to dance a whole routine in front of the rest of the class . . . I was always all over the place!!!

I missed my very last session as I had planned another girls' holiday to Bali for a week. It was fantastic; we stayed in a resort which had a beautiful beach but the most part of the hotel was surrounded by trees and bushes it actually looked like a jungle. One of the day out there I was walking back to my room and I saw a snake, it slithered off into one of the shrubs, and then another day when I was at the pool I opened up my towel and found snake skin inside it. Anita, Parveen and I also saw two kamodos fighting, which spooked us as we heard rustling in the bushes and all of a sudden they came running out chasing and fighting each other, there were lizards everywhere even in our room and they squeak, like mice, I never knew lizards made noise until then . . . it was definitely an experience!

Whilst in Bali I made a decision . . . I decided that I no longer wanted to work at the college anymore. I wasn't happy there and hadn't been for quite some time. I decided to hand in my resignation when I got back. I didn't have another job to go to but I knew that I just didn't want to be there anymore. It was the one aspect of my life that was extremely negative, and I wasn't happy about, so I knew that it was time to leave. I didn't know what I was going to do or when or where I would be working next . . . but my gut instinct just told me that I was going to be alright, and that this was now my time, my time to shine.

> "We know what we are, but know not what we may be."
> William Shakespeare

Choosing my Circle & Fighting For What I Believe In

At this point I realised that I had a lot of negative people around me, and although I had thought they were my friends in actual fact they were not. It was time to clear out the negativity from my world. I had sorted myself out bit by bit, and now it was time to fix everything else around me.

I started out with my facebook friends. If I had not been in communication with them for the past 6 months, I took them off as my friends. Next came people in my phone book. I had 156 people and then, after deleting a few I only had 127. I have found that those at work that pretended to be my friends really were not, and there were just a handful that were. I knew that when I left there would be very few people that I would still keep in contact with. The people that I found were bringing negativity in my world I had clean out of my life . . . it may have sounded harsh but this was my way of cleansing and starting all over again . . . it was a fresh start and all I wanted was positivity surrounding me and filling my world.

My new line manager, let's call him Hitler , who already had a bad reputation as you can tell by the name we had given him for being a bully, was about 4 years younger than me and was experienced and qualified. He was very cocky and arrogant; he could do no wrong and no one could tell him otherwise. The department I worked in before rivalled with the department I now work in so as you can imagine the first day was intense and was like walking into the lion's den. There were 5 of us who were transferred to this department and none of us felt comfortable, so much had gone on within the department.

We were coming up to the Christmas break which meant we had full two weeks off, and to be honest it couldn't come sooner; we were all counting down the days.

On the last day we usually finished work early but this year we were told that we have to stay and work to the very end even though every other department in the college had left during lunch . . . I didn't think that this was fair but we had no choice.

Unknown to me, Hitler decided that he would let everyone apart from 2 people go home early, and he decided that Mee Mee and I would have to stay. I was fuming when he told me that this is what he decided. I asked how he came about the decision to keep the both of us working and that it was not fair. He turned round and said "I am the manager and that is what I have decided,." I asked him again "Don't you think this is unfair? We are meant to be one team and we are being treated differently."

He then became annoyed and told me that was what he decided, period. I walked out of his office and decided to go to speak to his manager upstairs. As I walked off my colleagues, including Mee Mee, saw me and saw that I was annoyed. My face went red, I was so angry. I spoke to his manager and explained what had happened, I told him that we are meant to be a team and although I didn't mind staying until the end you cannot justify how some can go home early and others have to stay if we are a team.

He listened to what I had to say and was very calm about it and said that he could clearly see that there was an issue, and because of this the whole team would need to stay. I felt much better, and went to the toilets to cool off before returning to the department. How can Hitler possibly think that this was ok and moral? How can he think that I would just sit back and no do nothing it was so immoral and a bullying tactic clearly.

When I went back it was clear that he was told the rest of team would have to stay. He was storming around and slamming things on the table . . . how mature . . . and he was supposed to be my line manager, the one I was meant to trust and rely on for direction . . . tut tut!

Months went past and he seemed to have grown a liking to me and started to talk to me like a human being and asking me for my opinion and advise; soon after it was announced that I was now Team Leader. How did this happen?

It was our busiest time of year -- 'Bulk Enrolment.' This was in the summer every year where we would prepare for school leavers to come in and enrol in one of our courses. We had hundreds of people coming in and staff were expected to work extra hours anywhere between 8.30am- 9pm. There were days that were so busy that it was difficult to get a pee break let alone get an hour for lunch.

Hitler told me that staff could only have 45 minutes for lunch, and a few days later he cut it down again to only 30 minutes. This was difficult on the staff especially as they were working 12 hour shifts some days.

One day Hitler came up to me and told me that the team were not working hard enough, even though they were barely getting any breaks and working extremely long hours. He asked if he could cut it down to 20 minutes. As I was I was a representative for the union I told him that this was illegal and he could not expect staff to only have a 20 minute break. He then went on and told me that I needed to start swearing at staff if I wanted them to do what I wanted. I was shocked by this and I told him that I had no problem with staff taking direction from me, and if he seemed to be having this problem then clearly he needed to change the way he approached the staff. Then I walked off.

I could see from his reaction that he did appreciate my honesty but I had morals and this was completely out of order and does not make you a great manger. He clearly was wrong for this position and proved it many times.

We had temporary staff that were employed just for this busy season. I found out that Hitler had shouted at a temporary member of staff in front of everyone and then threatened him with physical abuse if the task was not done on time. For days I didn't know what to do. Should I approach Hitler about this or ignore it, as my brother was only working for another couple weeks?

I couldn't ignore it any longer and I had so many staff members approach me and complain about him. I decided to take action and went to HR. An investigation took place and Hitler was not working at the college for much longer. I had to do what was right and his behaviour had become worse because he had already gotten away with so much. I wasn't going to sit back and take it any longer, especially as the team's morale was so low and they were coming to me crying for help.

*"Failure will never overtake me if
my determination to succeed is strong enough."*
Og Mandino

Chapter 8
The Finale

Taking Risks

As I found a new passion in events but didn't have any experience except for the event that I organised and planned myself, I decided to volunteer my time. I signed up to the Mayor of London volunteer website, and soon found lots of events around London that I applied to work for. These events were held on the weekends, which meant I could still continue to work at the college during the week.

I worked at the Chinese New Year event in Trafalgar Square, a huge event with thousands of people attending. I also worked in Angel at an Arts Youth Centre where they were trying to promote. It was an up and coming centre the local community could attended. I was part of the planning of a theatre production, which we would advertise and people would buy tickets to come and see. I somehow wound up acting in this production and played several different characters. I even had my very own solo.

I was part of a project where we decided to produce a book for children and I was a part of helping out at the book launch in Parliament. I was involved in the animated documentary for children and did voiceovers for different characters which was extremely fun and very different . . . I never thought I would ever do anything like this.

Even though none of these opportunities was bringing me in any income, I was happy. Happy because I was doing things that got me excited again and working with people who were positive and also excited about their jobs.

As I was focusing on the positives around me and really related to The Secret I decided that I wanted to attended one of Dr Demartini's event in London. He is one of many people who has contributed to The Secret, and I thought it would be amazing to attend his event and hopefully meet him.

I told my coach about this as well as another girl that I was training with, after all my coach was the one that introduced me to The Secret. That evening all three of us met up prior to attending the event and my coach told me that she had invited a friend, Roxanne, along. she was very prim and proper and seemed very confident. Once the event had finished and we were walking out, Roxanne was talking about where she worked, and that they were looking for an events person. She asked me about my experience, skills and what kinds of things I was looking for. As I told her about my experience, she said that she would get back to me, and took my number.

I didn't think anything would come of it . . . I mean who just offers you a job like that on the spot when they don't even know you!

I handed my manager an envelope and he read my resignation. To my shock he looked at me and refused my resignation. My mouth dropped and my heart sank! A few days later another lot of voluntary redundancies were announced and people had to apply for it. I decided this was my way out.

Never Judge a Book by its Cover

> *"He who is not courageous enough to take risks will accomplish nothing in life."*
> Muhammad Ali

Having Doubts

Did I do the right thing leaving my job when I had no other job to go to? I kept falling in and out of doubt. People were looking at me as though I was mad because I didn't have another job to go to. Even my mum was worried. But looking for another job takes a lot of time, and I needed to leave the college in order to find the time to do this.

However, my dad told me that I needed to leave the college; that I had tried and was not getting anywhere. "Besides," he said, "all you do when you get home is complain about work, so it's probably best that you find something else."

As I had been getting totally different responses from my parents for a long while, I was battling myself . . . until I watched The Secret. Then it became clear as to what I had to do in order to be happy again, and eliminate what was making me unhappy. After I left, I felt free; like I could do almost anything that I wanted to do. Even though I had no idea how it was going to work out, and I knew I could be home for months before I found another job, but at the same time I knew that I would find something that I was passionate about. I knew I was going to be fine.

What needs to be understood is that you don't need to have everything planned, the what, who and when. You just need to be certain of what you want. Every time I felt like I was having doubts, I simply just shook it off and thought about what The Secret had taught me. I focused on the positives around me. I continued to write in my gratitude book. Not only did I write all the things I was grateful for, I also wrote about the things I wanted, as if I already had them. I started to believe in myself again. I stopped worrying about the future because I knew somehow it would all work out and I was going to do everything that I wanted, and be happy and content with every aspect of my life.

> *"The only limit to our realization of tomorrow will be our doubts of today."*
> Franklin D. Roosevelt

Wait . . . This could work!

I am now working in events, with positive people in a positive environment. The people that I work with are genuine people, and they are changing people's lives for the better. I feel like my dreams are coming true!!!

I have met many amazing people on the way, from different backgrounds and experiences. It's great to meet so many like-minded people who are motivated and determined. Many of them have come from nothing, and continued to believe in themselves to push for what they wanted.

I've never felt this happy and content. I'm finally in a place where I feel that I can do anything I want to do. I have found the courage to go travelling on my own, and I feel free, like I am floating in clouds. I rarely see my family due to my work schedule, but when I do see them the time spent is so much better, and everyone makes an effort.

One of the other goals that was on my vision board, but that I never mentioned until now, was to write a book ... and here I am! I have come to the end of writing my very first book.

Never Judge a Book by its Cover

If you have reached this point of my book, then you have now reached the end. I hope you have enjoyed it and that it has given you joy and the motivation to continue to pursue your dreams. Wow . . . This is Amazing!

"Start by doing what's necessary; then do what's possible; and suddenly you are doing the impossible."
Francis of Assisi

Made in the USA
Charleston, SC
28 April 2016